Third Eye Awakening

Guided Meditation to Open Your Third Eye

(Secrets of Third Eye Chakra Activation for Higher Consciousness)

Johnny Gause

Published By **Bella Frost**

Johnny Gause

All Rights Reserved

Third Eye Awakening: Guided Meditation to Open Your Third Eye (Secrets of Third Eye Chakra Activation for Higher Consciousness)

ISBN 978-1-7780570-3-8

No part of this guidebook shall be reproduced in any form without permission in writing from the publisher except in the case of brief quotations embodied in critical articles or reviews.

Legal & Disclaimer

The information contained in this book is not designed to replace or take the place of any form of medicine or professional medical advice. The information in this book has been provided for educational & entertainment purposes only.

The information contained in this book has been compiled from sources deemed reliable, and it is accurate to the best of the Author's knowledge; however, the Author cannot guarantee its accuracy and validity and cannot be held liable for any errors or omissions. Changes are periodically made to this book. You must consult your doctor or get professional medical advice before using any of the suggested remedies, techniques, or information in this book.

Upon using the information contained in this book, you agree to hold harmless the Author from and against any damages, costs, and expenses, including any legal fees potentially resulting from the application of any of the information provided by this guide. This disclaimer applies to any damages or injury caused by the use and application, whether directly or indirectly, of any advice or information presented, whether for breach of contract, tort, negligence, personal injury, criminal intent, or under any other cause of action.

You agree to accept all risks of using the information presented inside this book. You need to consult a professional medical practitioner in order to ensure you are both able and healthy enough to participate in this program.

Table Of Contents

Chapter 1: What Are Chakras? 1

Chapter 2: The Sixth Chakra - Ajna Chakra 21

Chapter 3: Activating The Third Eye Chakra 35

Chapter 4: The Health Benefits Of Energy Healing 45

Chapter 5: The Pineal Gland 65

Chapter 6: Sacral Chakra Healing 87

Chapter 7: Meaning Of The Third Eye .. 123

Chapter 1: What Are Chakras?

Chakras are subtle strength facilities placed in places of nerve plexuses. Chakra in Sanskrit manner "wheel." In our diffused frame, there are seven critical chakras, every of which corresponds to a degree of evolution. Each chakra is responsible for the embodiment of a person of high-quality spiritual features that most human beings are in an unmanifest country.

Chakras are the most famous elements of the precept of the subtle frame considering many authors interested by yoga, Tibetan Buddhism, Theosophy, and parapsychological research have supplied diverse descriptions of the chakras and feedback on them. Although the seven stages of samadhi are already stated in classical yogic sutras, the development of the concept of chakras probable began out out simplest with the appearance of tantric practices.

Often trembling, twitching, twisting, or vibration taking area within the regions of the chakras in humans in the course of a massage session or at some point of emotional or physical pressure. It seems that during the ones locations, there may be a block that does not permit power to transport uniformly throughout the body. It is possible that blocks are created with the useful resource of unresolved troubles or intellectual issues related to chakras. This is associated with physical problems in the functioning of the organs of the human body for the reason that maximum of the chakras manipulate the art work of sure organs.

Another phenomenon that may be correlated with the action of the electricity of the chakras is the spontaneous incidence of precise snap shots, sounds, and logos, which in tantric cosmology are taken into consideration to be inherent in all chakras. Their have a look at some level in catastrophe situations can offer facts associated with those problems that need to be resolved, or mean the location of the body, focusing on as a manner to supply the best impact. For those reasons, it is useful to have an idea of the chakra tool, which is printed right proper here - in widespread terms.

Chakras are referred to as such objects as neurohormonal mechanisms of controlling zones of the frame; multidimensional passages through which innovative forces go with the float among 3 our bodies; centers of the frame's electricity machine; energy funnels; intermediaries that switch electricity from one measurement to 3 different; "interdimensional transforming systems that may be managed with the useful resource of idea and which flip rely into energy" (Joy); facilities of subtle forces, cosmic interest and prana technology.

According to Goswami, the Bindu of the chakras inside the sphere of pranic power play the identical position as atoms inside the fabric sphere. He stated: "A shifting or energetic pranic pressure concentrates and gathers to shape petals of Bindu at numerous factors within the frame, which in yoga are known as chakras, or lotuses. This formation begins offevolved with the Sahasrara chakra and continues with the decrease chakras with how human attention is fashioned and his fabric body. All this is invisible to the naked eye. The chakras function on a supermaterial degree. "

Usually, the chakras are taken into consideration the connecting hyperlink among all kinds of sports activities of the causal, diffused, and gross our our bodies. From them come the vritti (waves of mind), further to distinctive energies which may be disbursed at a few level in the frame. Therefore, each of them is attributed to high-quality emotions and houses. If we take the chakras as the principle converters and transmitters of energy among our bodies, it becomes clean that developing the anxiety of recognition and strength is a effective greater load on the chakra device. Often, chakras are defined as lotuses transferring from backside to top with energy rising via them.

The chakras include all the untangled nodes and troubles of a person's personal and emotional lifestyles, and inside the direction of religious transformation, they could make contributions to the mixture of styles of popularity which might be extra feature of a unifying characteristic and which might be much less ego-oriented.

There are seven principal chakras and forty three a whole lot a great deal much less critical, which can be attributed to many houses in unique texts. It is believed that at some stage inside the day, prana alternately dominates in wonderful chakras in line with a sixty-minute rhythm. Several styles of symbols are related to each of the principle chakras. The latter encompass an animal personifying the diffused forces that manage the chakra; God, which denotes one of the forces of divine manifestation; a goddess who suggests the form of electricity placed at this thing. Other symbols denote the dominant element and one of the 5 senses associated with this chakra. Meditation on every chakra awakens the power of the goddess who is there, for you to open up specific divine possibilities for man. Lotus petals constitute various trends, emotional dispositions, and opportunities.

The First Chakra - Muladhara Chakra

Located almost on the very forestall of the spine and touching the anus and testicles or cervix, this chakra is precise because the 4-petaled lotus, whose petals constitute ultimate happiness, innate bliss, the bliss of crew spirit and bliss of courage and energy. She is considered a contemplated photograph of the crown chakra at the physical degree, and consequently her petals are really glad. The nature of this chakra is same to Brahman, the modern precept of the universe. We can expect that it preserves the material shape of the frame and that its underlying information and potentials of human evolution are hidden.

This is the inspiration and assist of the body, and its safety and self-safety depend upon its ordinary functioning. This chakra corresponds to the detail earth, orange-red shade, and feel of odor. An elephant with a black stripe throughout the neck is its photograph and represents earthly tendencies: electricity, firmness, balance and manual, those characteristics are represented via the yellow square inscribed in the circle of yantra or mandala depicting this chakra. It additionally has a triangle referred to as Tripura and represents will, records, and movement.

Muladhara impacts the rectum, kidneys, sperm accumulation, and the genitals, in addition to bones, pores and pores and skin, muscle mass, nerves, and hair. It is related to the prevalence of physiological problems which incorporates hemorrhoids, constipation, sciatica, and prostate illnesses. It is associated with a revel in of fragrance, and its vibration motives boom or contraction of the lungs.

Mishra writes that via pratyahara (distraction of the senses), anger, lust, and greed are curbed in this chakra. Longing and depression also are taken into consideration symptoms and signs and signs of an imbalance in it.

Meditation in this chakra establishes control over attachments to luxurious, lies, pleasure, envy, and narcissism. Pandit said that the Muladhara controls bodily or unconscious actions or impulses. In the yantra (the symbolic image of the chakra), there may be a blood-pink triangle of hearth that inflates the kandarpa vayu, the purpose of sexual arousal, that is critical for reproducing the human race. Motoyama wrote that when this chakra awakens, it releases suppressed emotions explosively, that would result in the emergence of excessive irritability and mental instability in someone, a violation of sleep styles, excitability.

Meditation on the god of this chakra, Mahadeva, who sits along together with his face, have become again, cleanses from sins. Brahma, the god of absolute modern energy, furthermore offers this chakra the goddess Dakini Shakti, the power of introduction. If you repeat the mul mantra, at the identical time as keeping the serenity of the mind and devotion and focusing on this chakra, then you could wake up her goddess. In yoga cosmology, precisely underneath this chakra is the Kundalini power, curled up in three and a half turns. Yogis consider that that is wherein the confluence of sushumna (nadi, wearing the circulate of existence), Vajra Nadi (nadi carrying the electrical go with the flow), and Brahma Nadi (sound waft or motion of spirit) merge.

The Second Chakra - Svadhishthana Chakra

Located barely above the muladhara at the lowest of the penis, or in the center of the lower again, this chakra is associated with the conquest of water; its symbols are the crescent and the god Vishnu, nourishing the precept of the universe. Its colour is commonly considered red or scarlet and once in a while - white. Rakini Shakti, a darkish blue goddess with three pink eyes and four arms, from whose nose blood flows, consists of the power of this chakra. She holds in her palms a trident, a lotus, a drum, and a chisel. A mild gray or green sea monster reminiscent of a crocodile is an animal image of the chakra, it personifies dominance over the ocean and indicates a connection with the unconscious. By meditating on this chakra, someone defeats the factors.

She has six petals, which constitute the highbrow tendencies of forget about about, numbness, credulity, suspicion, preference for destruction and cruelty, and additionally represent six nerves related to the colon, rectum, kidneys, bladder, genitals, and testicles. This chakra promotes the circulate of liquid materials within the body, their conservation, and vitamins; it is also considered a middle of the heterosexual orientation of a person.

Mishra wrote that this chakra controls, controls, and nourishes the ft. By specializing in it, someone feels a magnetic pulsation, movement, and vibration and may remove all of the unpleasant sensations, pains, and ailments in his legs. Other situations associated with this chakra consist of sexual troubles, diabetes, kidney and bladder sicknesses. By meditating on it, a person is freed from egoistic feelings, small impulses, and goals. The equanimity and serenity of the thoughts enlarge. The everyday functioning of the Svadhishthana is related to a experience of self-self guarantee and properly-being, and with the frustrations in her artwork, unhappiness, addiction, and tension. This chakra is also related to a experience of flavor and language. According to 3 tantras, if you want to apprehend it, someone want to grasp the language.

The Third Chakra - Manipura Chakra

Located above Svadvishthana opposite the navel, Manipura is associated with Rudra, a god who distributes objects and creates fear, personifying the damaging precept of the universe (the arena of the mind). The goddess Lakini Shakti, carrying yellow clothes, is called the benefactress of the universe, and one of the texts describes that she loves animal meat, her chest is blanketed with blood, and fats is dripping from her lips. The animal photo is a ram, an animal sacrificed, which personifies the want to sacrifice addictions, impulsive urges, and different sturdy emotions.

Concentration over manipura brings comprehension of feces or everlasting time. Perhaps this level of openness may be associated with the pass decrease lower back of reminiscences of different lives or states that take human beings beyond the limits of recognition created by using time. This chakra is also associated with manipulate of warmth and directs the agni, the fiery principle, that's concept to control the creature's unbridled movements and digestive gadget. Manipura controls the internal organs of the belly, specifically, the functioning of the stomach, liver, and massive gut, and is associated with a section of the crucial nerve-racking system placed above the lumbar region. Some say that focusing on this middle can remedy diseases of the stomach organs, specially if you meditate on the crimson shade in it.

Ten petals that convey the developments of disgrace, treachery, envy, desire, drowsiness, despondency, shallowness, delusion, disgust, and fear make up this chakra. However, regular with one of the tantric texts, even as a yogi meditates on this chakra and pronounces a mul mantra, he's continuously in a remarkable temper and illnesses cannot penetrate his / her body. Such a yogi can input into the our our bodies of others and notice siddhas (saints and instructors of yoga), can, at a glance, determine the characteristics of material gadgets and spot items underground. It is apparent why this chakra is so regularly associated with gaining power and locating a exquisite area within the international. It is also a place of hara that one specializes in during a few Zen meditations. This interest offers rise to a sense of balance and resilience in the being,

The putting in place of this chakra requires the participation of the eyes and such manipulate over their movements in order that they do no longer for a second come off the center placed the various eyebrows.

The Fourth Chakra - Anahata Chakra

The vicinity of the coronary coronary heart chakra is normally indicated opposite the middle line strolling among the nipples, however once in a while it's far moved barely to the proper of the sternum, despite the fact that now not without delay above the coronary coronary heart. It is associated with the conquest of the element of air, in addition to with the coronary coronary heart and nada, the sound of cosmic cognizance. By meditating on this middle, you may revel in how the power flows in the course of the whole nervous machine as though it is entire of magnetism. Many traditions of spiritual improvement emphasize the significance of the heart chakra because the chakra that wishes to be wakened within the first place in order to revel in a spiritual awakening due to the fact it's miles proper here that the energies of the lower and upper stages of attention merge, which represent intersecting triangles. In addition, anahata, combining the energies of various chakras, moreover connects the left and proper facets of the body, the characteristics of yin and yang.

Isha is the god of this chakra; he sits on a black antelope or gazelle, which symbolizes the rate and simplicity of air. Isha is the very first-class God, endowed with complete yogic energy, omniscient, and omnipresent. It is white and symbolizes purity; it has 3 eyes; the 1/3 represents know-how of samadhi. When its form arises in the direction of meditation, fears disappear, and focus intensifies.

The yantra pix of the coronary heart chakra include intersecting triangles, inner which might be a colourful golden creature and Kakini Shakti, the lightning-colored goddess who radiates slight and delight. Kakini is called the keeper of the doorways of Anahata and meditating on it; someone learns to stabilize prana and do away with boundaries at the way to Isha. When the goddess is purple, it manner that her electricity is used to control pranic electricity; at the same time as she is white, she is Isha consciousness.

The twelve scarlet petals related to Anahata represent ready, pleasure, diligence, affection, hypocrisy, vulnerable thing, selfishness, separation, greed, fraud, indecision, and regret. Meditation on this chakra brings possession of sound, and if you say the mul mantra during meditation, you're greater organized to recognize God, as someone earnings manipulate over his emotions, particularly, reducing the texture of touch. Then, as they'll be pronouncing, no longer a single preference will live unfulfilled -

then a person will all of the time plunge proper proper into a country of bliss.

If you appearance from a one-of-a-type difficulty of view, we will assume that, freed from attachment to all "coronary coronary heart" desires (as evidenced by the use of the traits embodied within the petals), a person income the capacity to distract the senses from all worldly subjects and because of this collect a rustic of bliss first for brief periods and then all the time.

The trends of compassion, beauty, and unconditional love are symptoms of the balanced functioning of this chakra. Indifference, passivity, and disappointment are symptoms of an imbalance — a few authors accomplice arthritis and respiratory problems with cardiac chakra, in addition to cardiovascular disorder and high blood strain.

The beginning of this chakra is considered viable with the assist of the pores and pores and skin; that is, you want to surpass the enjoy of contact, this is finished via manner of achieving manipulate over sensory belief through kumbhaka (breath-maintaining). A not unusual way to discover the power of anahata is a meditation on it with the simultaneous presentation of mild or breathing in and respiratory out air from it.

The Fifth Chakra - Vishuddha Chakra

Located inside the throat is the vishuddhi lotus - gray or silver (and on occasion smoky purple) and has 16 petals. They consist of seven musical notes, poison and nectar, and 7 "invocations," which can be used to guard in the course of demons, in the direction of sacrifices, to mild sacred lights, to provide dedication, to bless and glorify. Here start the priestly or occult powers related to the forces of projection or expression. This chakra is likewise related to the conquest of the etheric state of rely (vicinity). This chakra is generally related to innovative hobby and suggestion, further to receiving ethical steerage, specially whilst in contact with an inexhaustible source of "grace." A individual starts offevolved to enjoy that the inner giver and taker are one and the identical.

The god of this chakra is Shiva in a half male, half of of woman form (Ardhanarishvara), he sits on a white elephant, and with him is the 4-armed yellow Shakini Shakti (goddess). He owns hundreds of statistics. She rules inside the state of the moon over insignificant secrets and techniques and strategies and techniques.

Vishuddha controls both fingers and is the middle of pratyahara or distraction of the senses. When someone focuses interest right here, he loses his fingers sensitivity to warmness, cold, ache, pressure, touch, and temperature. Tantras say that the gadgets of this chakra are ears, they may be carried out within the sort of manner that the noise of the world does not distract, and best one sound is heard: both nada (the sound of

Ohms is of plenty much less intensity) or the decision of God. Meditation on this chakra leads one to the brink of extraordinary liberation.

Chapter 2: The Sixth Chakra - Ajna Chakra

Ajna is positioned above the nostril among the eyebrows is the supply of nerve flows, truly certainly one of which passes thru the eyes, and the alternative via the mid-brain. There are 3 fundamental nadi (sushumna, ida, and pingala). The potential to create and gain is generated via highbrow waves emanating from this factor. This chakra controls the internal imaginative and prescient and dynamic interest of the selection and information. This "zero.33 eye" in plenty of cultures is associated with mild, internal understanding, intuition, and mediumistic abilties. The discovery of these skills involves the mixing of each intellectual and emotional poles.

The goddess of ajna is the six-confronted and 6-armed Hakini Shakti; she personifies the five thoughts concentrated inside the decrease chakras and the offers of the ajna chakra. When its coloration is described as purple, then the expertise of Kundalini is actually wakened; at the same time as she is white, she represents a nation of relaxation; even as it's far darkish blue, it's miles at the verge of transitioning into a shapeless kingdom. When visible in a mixture of white, red, and black hues, she indicates a mixture of 3 gunas: sattva (harmonious popularity), rajas (hobby) and tamas (inertia).

Meditation in this center brings visions of the very high-quality fact, yogic powers, liberation from all Sanskars, and in the long run awareness, higher facts. This is the middle of individual attention, which through pratyahara, may be extended to regular. Ajna is frequently known as guiding all different chakras, and a few yogis recommend to pay interest simplest on it, or first of all, in advance than awakening energies in different facilities. Thus, the development of the features inherent in all previous chakras can be stimulated, and so the student can attain a country of nondual focus. It is assumed that it is not feasible to completely master the lower chakras in advance than Ajna is awakened.

The Seventh Chakra - Sahasrara Chakra

According to a few texts, sahasrara is located on the top of the top inside the thoughts; others trust that it's far above the bodily frame and is equal with Parabrahma, the final writer. Her lotus has a thousand petals, five of which represent all the letters of the Sanskrit alphabet. Samadhi, felt via this chakra, is a whole merger with existence, without the boundaries of ego-attention within the frame. (Although there are yoga systems in which particular tiers of chakras are indicated, extending further past the bodily body and to this primary diploma of higher recognition.)

Parabrahma governs this center, symbolized with the aid of way of the use of the triangle of focus, that is called Vija - that is each different call for the divine essence of sat-chit-ananda. It represents overcoming barriers and merging with emptiness or the Upper Light out of doors the shape, a country which, in keeping with most yogic sacred books and the saying of the saints, a person cannot describe.

Meditating here, consistent with Bose and Haldor, a person crosses the limits of advent, safety, and destruction and may taste the sweet nectar (amrita) flowing in a non-stop motion from sahasrara. A character is freed, all Sanskars are destroyed, after which he isn't difficulty to either starting or loss of life. At this diploma of awakening, man or woman identity disappears forever, and a person is identified with a higher popularity. (It is critical to do not forget that after yogis communicate about the united states of immortality, they normally do not imply that someone will certainly in no manner depart the frame, but rather propose that conscious fusion with the countless is executed all the time and could not be destroyed with the lack of existence of the frame).

Opening Your Third Eye

The 1/three eye is home to a person's 6th revel in. When it is truly open and balanced, you end up extra intuitive and advantage better knowledge. It isn't that clean to open the 0.33 eye chakra and maximum human beings find it tough.

Prepare your self first with the resource of doing the following steps:

1. Nurture silence. Find processes that will help you in fostering the silence of the thoughts. You can attempt getting centered on an art or undertaking, being one with nature, or through meditation. It is vital that your mind remains calm just so it received't miss any message coming from the opposite realm.

2. Develop your instinct. You ought to exercise the intuitive techniques to make it much less difficult as a manner to understand the messages and visions you'll be getting. Have amusing within the manner and do now not sense careworn with the obligations concerned. Learn a manner to test tarot playing cards and horoscope and get acquainted with the meanings of goals.

three. Let your creativity go together with the go together with the flow. You ought to find tactics to loosen your rational thoughts. Get inspired in trying out new hobbies, crafts, and arts. You don't have to be best and you don't want to pressure your self to provide you some trouble all of the time. You certainly need to revel in the method and permit your imagination take you to everywhere it leads you. The exercise will calm your thoughts, so one can growth the capability of your 1/three eye to spread and improve.

four. Be grounded all of the time. This is the maximum important basis so that you can assist you to understand your extrasensory perceptions in reality. If you aren't grounded, you will probable experience stressed and disturbed through the pix and thoughts as a manner to come back lower back to you. It permits in establishing the subtle channels of belief. This will keep away from the not unusual horrible effects of having an open 0.33 eye.

Once you've got organized your self for what is ready to show up, you may perform smooth however powerful sports activities sports to aid the hole of your 6th chakra. Here are a number of the sporting sports as a way to assist in boosting your intuitive power center:

Reflect and rest under the moonlight. The moderate coming from the moon has similar trends to the mild of your intuitive middle.

The critical feature of your zero.33 eye is instinct so constantly discover strategies to exercise this ability.

Strengthen the energy coming from the chakras beneficial in unlocking the powers of your 1/three eye and in preserving it balanced, which include the first and throat chakras.

Embrace silence because of the reality this is your gate to pay attention the whisper of the zero.33 eye's expertise.

Contemplate and meditate.

Cultivate your psychic skills.

Learn a manner to artwork with spirit guides.

Always be curious about the whole lot round you, which encompass symbols and their meanings.

The Role of the Pineal Gland in Awakening the Third Eye

The feature of the 0.33 eye is associated with each the pineal and pituitary glands. The pituitary gland is referred to as the human frame's draw close gland due to the truth it's far answerable for controlling one-of-a-type glands and the manner they produce hormones. The pineal gland, as an opportunity, is located on the identical degree due to the fact the eyes and right at the center of the mind. It is positioned inside the back of and above the pituitary gland.

Modern metaphysics and yogic traditions view the pineal gland due to the fact the seat of the soul and supply of psychic powers, extrasensory belief, and mystical reports. The capabilities of the gland are similar to the cycles of mild and darkness.

Here are the sports activities activities which you have to do to decorate the potential of the pineal gland in awakening your 1/3 eye:

Meditate. It kindles the a part of the mind that enhances the pineal gland and permits in retaining the stability of your fearful tool.

Step outside and bask within the glory of light.

Find a while to spend in complete darkness. It stimulates the producing of the pineal gland's hormones and maintains it active and healthful.

Eat nutritional supplements and food that help in retaining the pineal gland healthful.

The pineal gland gets greater blood go with the flow than every other organs inside the frame and it's far surrounded with highly charged cerebrospinal fluid. It is likewise a rich supply of melatonin and is stated to contain the first-rate consciousness of energy.

Melatonin is a appeared antioxidant and anti-stress and anti-developing antique agent. It influences someone's excellent and length of sleep, circadian rhythms, immune function, and temper. Light and darkness have an impact on the pineal gland's production of melatonin. Light prevents the producing and it is activated via darkness.

Once melatonin is launched into the tool, it circulates to the thoughts via the blood that surrounds the pineal gland earlier than it's far going into the blood vessels to get allotted at a few stage inside the frame.

It is crucial that you keep the pineal gland wholesome and activated as it has religious connections. This tiny pine-cone-common gland has been preserved one by one with the beneficial useful resource of ancient Egyptians inside the route of the mummification method. It is also used as an artifact in lots of ancient traditions wherein it has been associated with immortality and enlightenment. Its form symbolizes the right series of Fibonacci because it represents advent and growth.

This gland is likewise the important thing to starting the 1/3 eye. Here are some of the crucial techniques that you could look at to set off the pineal gland:

1. Tapping. Gently faucet your forehead in which the 1/three eye chakra is located. The vibration turns on the pineal gland, stimulates the pituitary gland, and awakens the hypothalamus.

2. Breathing. Proper respiration will boom the efficiency of cerebrospinal fluid or CSF. Learn the remarkable breathing practices that increase the go with the go with the flow of CSF.

3. Squeezing. The pituitary gland is activated when you squeeze your eyes. To stimulate cranial pumps and neck, flow into your jaw via manner of sucking your cheeks. As the

perineum and anal sphincter agreement, vibrations are despatched to the muscular tissues surrounding the pelvic ground. The vibration will then float up the backbone to the occiput in advance than moving to the mid part of the pinnacle to prompt each the pituitary and pineal glands.

4. Toning. Also called chanting, it energizes the CSF and activates the pineal and other glands within the technique.

5. Smiling and giggling. Your coronary coronary coronary heart and crown open up whilst you smile. As a result, extra moderate is capable of penetrate and it'll increase the vibration of the organs. Smiling and giggling additionally assist your frame lighten up and decrease pressure, permitting an excellent float of chi or electricity at some level within the body. Relaxation furthermore boosts the blood go with the go with the flow, which

helps in activating the pineal gland. Laughing is commonly useful to fitness as it triggers the discharge of the hormones that assist in selling the emotions of nicely-being, called endorphins.

6. Spending time in darkness. Darkness boosts melatonin manufacturing. Once launched, it turns on the pineal gland and boosts the manufacturing of pinoline and DMT.

7. Pressing. Feel the roof of your mouth and press your tongue in it. The easy project activates the pituitary gland and inside the system, activates the pineal gland and hypothalamus through the chemical and bodily connections.

eight. Focus. Bring your attention to the location of some thing you want to activate and your power will go with the drift toward that direction.

9. Spiraling movements. These actions embody spinning the Tai Chi photo or pakua a good way to form an electromagnetic area and produce more energy to the CSF. It will then beautify the heart area's power and prompt the pineal gland.

Chapter 3: Activating The Third Eye Chakra

When the 1/three eye is open and balanced, your interest and attention enhance and also you turn out to be greater intuitive and reliant. Here are some practices to conform with to hone such skills via activating the 0.33 eye chakra:

1. Practice conscious respiration. It calms the thoughts, opens and cleanses the zero.33 eye, and lets in in balancing the chakra tool.

2. Add the colours consultant of the 0.33 eye chakra in your surroundings. You can use clothes with the sunglasses of the color indigo or fill your office or domestic with accents in colours of the same sun shades.

three. Add end result and greens in the hues of crimson and natural blue. You can eat the fruits sparkling or flip them into a beverage.

four. Always discover time to exercise 1/3 eye meditation. Engage your 1/three eye on every occasion you've got were given time. This can without issues be finished through meditation and visualization. Sit somewhere quiet, close to your eyes, and visualize a purple or blue ball electricity inside the location of your 1/3 eye. Hold that picture as plenty as you may by means of the use of using concentrating. The hobby will open up the energy middle and it's going to furthermore help in healing and balancing the chakra.

five. Keep a dream journal. You ought to exercising remembering your desires and analyzing approximately their meanings.

6. Use essential oils with slight fragrances to open, cleanse, and balance the chakras. You can use one or a combination of any of the following oils to heal and activate your 1/3 eye chakra:

Nutmeg

Grapefruit

Roman or German Chamomile

Myrrh

Sandalwood

Third Eye Chakra Stones

You can use numerous gems, crystals, and recovery stones to open, stability, and heal your chakra machine. These recuperation stones have one-of-a-kind houses and characteristic their non-public precise vibrational power frequency. Here are some of the crystals and stones that you could use, which includes their cause and because of this:

1. Black Obsidian. This semi-precious stone is to be had in colour black. It receives rid of chakra blockages and negativity. It additionally lets in in enhancing your emotional control. The stone is used for stability and stimulation.

2. Purple Fluorite. This semi-precious stone boosts recognition and highbrow readability. It moreover promotes intuit and dispels negativity. The stone is used for stability and stimulation.

three. Moldavite. This semi-valuable stone comes in shade dark inexperienced. It complements dream and makes it less difficult if you want to recall them. It has the ability to restore the stability of the complete chakra tool. It is also applied in clearing negativity, restoring stability, stimulating, and cleaning.

4. Amethyst. The coloration of this valuable stone varies from light to darkish solar shades of purple. It is considered as a restoration stone that protects you from damage, heals, and gives expertise. It is also utilized in restoring stability, stimulating, and in organising your 1/three eye.

Chakra Meditation

Maybe you take into account reflection an instance of sitting leg over leg and murmuring to oneself. All topics taken into consideration; this isn't always all what contemplation is ready. You will discover a big style of styles of contemplation that assist you in unwinding and diminishing stress. Chakra is a particular form of reflected picture which begins from Hindu convictions. Today, the forte of chakra meditated image has unfold to each edge of the globe.

Chakra Meditation is a shape of mirrored image that contains pretty a few unwinding approaches targeting bringing parity, unwinding and prosperity to the chakras. "Chakra" is an antiquated Sanskrit phrase that indicates vortex or wheel that can be followed back to India.

Chakras are the human body's seven number one power focuses with each one concerning singular organs that administer our specific body elements in addition to awesome areas of the thoughts. They are positioned alongside a hormonal organ along the human spinal segment.

Chakras can wind up blocked and if even one of the 7 Chakras in the long run subsequently ends up blocked, it units us up for physical and passionate an problem that is some problem no person desires.

How Do Chakra Meditation Techniques Work?

Our awesome and perplexing universe circulates its brilliant existence-power strength to the earth and to our organs and organs located within the direction of the frame and circulatory device. This life-energy electricity is key so that you can obtaining splendid prosperity and well-being. It's preferred that for the cause that chakras are interrelated, they intently affect each other, through looking for to perform the appropriate diploma of equalization.

Make Each Cell in Your Body Stir and Celebrate!

A big element parents has lively squares and awkward nature sincerely as strength attacking propensities that hold us from getting to our entire essentialness, which leads us to sense depleted, dispersed, silly... even sick.

The Benefits of Meditation

In the occasion that new to meditation, questions regarding a capability to do it is able to ground, citing issues like "How ought to I recall nothing?" or issues like "I can not do this." It can appear like uncommon to attempt to discharge ourselves from the pending awful troubles in lifestyles by using the use of way of a what may additionally moreover look like a honest demonstration of sitting idle, in particular at the equal time as compelling passionate battles can mist our psyche.

It thoroughly can be difficult to easy your head while the type of fantastic quantity of weight from the outdoor international is through using all money owed pulling you down, but is substantially often essential for the duration of those unsightly ranges during normal life. When I began out ruminating, every other factor of view on existence conquered me. These are simplest multiple proposals from an lively tenderfoot which could permit someone to start a remunerating ordinary as regards to reflection and mindfulness.

Checking via breaths, one practice that has helped me hold my brain inside the outstanding spot even as reflecting is to check in some unspecified time inside the future of breaths. As I breathe in, I test till I've finished breathing in, with the useful resource of and huge spherical 8 for me, however may be something relying upon how short or mild you tally. As I breathe out, I tally to a similar amount, arriving at 8 when I've finished my breath out. Rehashing this device, I tally to 8 breathing in via my nose and after that considering to 8 I breathe out thru my mouth.

Cool air in/warmth allow some bypass into. I simply have likewise belief that it changed into gainful to reputation on my breaths as cool, excessive fine power filling my lungs and leaving as heat, terrible energy that has been stockpiled inner being discharged. Every breath is imagined, envisioning the superb, new cloud streaming in through my nostril and pushing the bad, stale cloud out as I breathe out via my mouth.

Concentrate on a solitary object. Another schooling that may be applied to encourage contemplation is to pay interest on a solitary article. The object may be anything. I maximum normally photograph a solitary slight lit in a dim live with no longer something else around. I watch it glint as contemplations go through my mind, aware about them however giving no consideration. As I get it, this sort of contemplation has actually been carried out to help with getting better specific quantities of the body.

Use sound for ruminating. A bit masses, but some thing that has helped me out masses, playing a sound can help with "timing " intervals, releasing me of considering to what amount I've been thinking. Here and there the usage of sound can get you greater profound, faster, but, I absolutely have a houseful with 5 kids, so setting on earphones and protecting up for twenty minutes is every so often the principle direction for me to art work on considering.

Practice every day. The more and more you accomplish some factor, the much less difficult and less complicated it gets. This stays regular for reflected picture, as nicely. Doing it continually builds up a valid propensity for taking a critical destroy and spotting the triumphing, excessively successfully unnoticed with our bustling timetables in this point in time. Practice each day and spot what opens up for you.

I'm though new to the act of reflected picture, so I comprehend the anxiety with newness. Be that as it is able to, I can't neglect the advantages of mirrored picture as they may be look at and enjoy for myself, further helping the concept we're in rate of our non-public situation. Also, as I preserve with my ordinary nearly approximately contemplation, I am charmingly astonished through the outstanding strength I experience while placing apart the try to find myself.

Chapter 4: The Health Benefits Of Energy Healing

It's extremely fascinating to be aware of that dependent on a disbursed American Heart Association's exam in November of 2012 approximately the effect of stress decrease responsibilities using mirrored image the discoveries examined that contemplation notably lessens stroke, cardiovascular failure, passing, outrage levels and the risks associated with coronary supply course infection.

The aftereffects of the program are very remarkable with the people who contemplated times regular with day for instances of 20 mins every day. They had the selection to lower coronary episode and stroke risks thru forty eight percentage. Furthermore, they likewise diminished their annoyance stages. It's exciting to take note of that the extra non-forestall the contemplation training, the better the great clinical blessings for the individuals.

Adapting to regular outrage could be very adverse to the brain and body. There are nice topics that one want to relinquish, or leave if there can be no preference for trade. To test with one model, toxic connections are not certainly lethal; they are a quandary to improving.

Chakra Meditation Music and Chakra Colors to Meditate

Music is every other control that is moreover executed in adjusting the chakras. Notwithstanding the tune, the leader has included severa amazing and amazing images. These chakra electricity colors are likewise a massive mending phase.

A case of chakra sunglasses includes inexperienced which identifies with the substance and discharges simply stifled harm. Another effective shading is indigo for the zero.33 eye that encourages us to appearance flawlessness no matter what. Blue is likewise carried out with throat chakra mirrored photograph and the declaration of truth via discourse.

Different strategies used to help mirrored photo contain guided symbolism, body unwinding, belief and respiratory techniques. Regardless of whether or no longer you understand it or no longer, your Chakras are grinding away indoors your body typically. They effect your intellectual virtually as your bodily state. By giving splendid attention to these zones, you may effect them to decorate positive factors of your life.

Meditation is a skill that can be found out and honed, much like a few different capability we attempt our hand at. It does no longer require any unique competencies. On the other hand, it additionally needs to be approached with out skepticism.

If you're new to meditation, you may experience a piece awkward and uncomfortable on the start. However, the bulk of people who experience the fun of meditation short discover ways to love it as a calming and enriching activity.

Meditation is largely an age-vintage practice hooked up in historic Indian traditions. It is practiced with the intention of beginning the thoughts for deeper intuition and belief. There are also several very powerful meditations superior mainly to open the 1/3 eye and pork up the pineal gland.

Meditation also allows you control your mind and your mind, placing you, because the proponents of Buddhism do not forget, in control of your life. This is a sincerely empowering present to have. So many stuff in life are out of our manage—but by way of manner of way of analyzing to govern our thoughts, we are able to reply to conditions because it need to be and gently and make higher alternatives. This talent becomes even more mentioned whilst your 1/3 eye chakra is wakened.

Meditation develops readability and improves interest and is probably one of the satisfactory methods to alleviate strain. These are just a few of the blessings of meditation. All of the bodily and intellectual blessings—as well as the research that confirms them—are surely too numerous to listing proper here.

How does Meditation Work?

When you meditate, your mind enters into an alpha wavelength nation, (which isn't always just like the regular beta wavelength u . S . That the mind resonates with). In this quiet and cushty united states of america, the mind will become greater open to receiving diffused messages and insights from our 0.33 eye. The ordinary exercise of meditation allows you to go into increasingly without difficulty into the alpha wavelength united states and over the years, you can accumulate deeper knowledge, expertise, and statistics from the non-bodily realm. It moreover allows improve spiritual gadgets.

Types of Meditation

The varieties of meditation are diverse and numerous. Zen meditation, Vispana meditation, mindfulness meditation, transcendental meditation, Taoist meditation, and mantra meditation are some of the most popular. There is also a sort of meditation for nearly something, from relieving pain and strain to meeting your better publications. But ideally, meditation want to be approached with the goal of attaining internal calm and deeper interest—and the sheer bliss of just being capable of overlook approximately the world and lighten up.

Meditations for the Third Eye

Meditation permits us to update off the questioning, logical mind. When the thoughts is quietened and enters an alpha diploma wavelength u . S . A ., it then turns into a filter out for subtle insights and messages from the 1/three eye.

All forms of meditation are effective for establishing the 1/three eye. Guided meditation and any form of mindfulness meditation will work thoroughly. However, the subsequent are the maximum effective for starting and nurturing the zero.33 eye.

Meditation 1: Trataka Meditation

This is an historic meditation derived from the Tantra and Hatha yoga practices. In Sanskrit, Trataka way "to gaze" or "to appearance."

● This meditation calls a good way to sit perfectly although on the floor with legs crossed inside the lotus feature. If this is not snug, take a seat down in a proper away-sponsored chair in which you could maintain your spine straight away.

● Close your eyes and breathe deeply from your belly for 2-to-3 mins till your body is without a doubt relaxed.

● Focus deeply at the vicinity of your 1/3 eye chakra. Continue to attention at the area for some moments.

● With every of your eyes however closed, draw them upwards inside the route of the inner eye chakra as if you are looking at it. You may also experience a pressure on your eyes as you try to hold them in that function. You will apprehend that it's miles the right position while you enjoy your eyes "lock" barely above the bridge of your nostril, and the area does not experience too strained.

• Keep your closed eyes in that function and slowly start counting backward from a hundred (with approximately seconds amongst every consider).

• Keep your closed eyes focused at the 1/three eye chakra till you've got completed counting backward to 0.

• Draw your eyes again to their everyday function and breathe deeply three instances to ground yourself. Allow your eyes to move again to their regular motion.

• Feel your self turn out to be grounded and open your eyes. The meditation need to very last amongst ten-to-fifteen minutes.

Some people document that once doing this meditation, they could truely see their thoughts as even though seeing a dream. You can also experience warmth in the location of the internal eye, which suggests that it is attracting power. In addition, not great is this a completely powerful meditation for awakening the 1/three eye, however it is also a wonderful workout that continues the eyes wholesome.

Note: This meditation should be practiced moderately to save you the over-activation of the 0.33 eye chakra. Once every week might be enough to keep the whole thing in stability.

Meditation 2: Body Scan Meditation for Third Eye Intuition

This meditation is particularly orientated in the path of developing your intuition thru the 0.33 eye chakra.

- Sit in a snug characteristic in conjunction with your decrease lower again right away.

- Close your eyes and do the aware respiratory exercising a good way to ground yourself. This want to take -to-3 mins, or until all of the anxiety is launched out of your body and also you sense absolutely comfortable.

- Start the frame test from the very pinnacle of your head or the crown chakra. Focus on this area until you begin to phrase the sensations there. This is probably tingling, pressure, a moderate warm temperature, burning, or humming. Don't fear if you do now not experience a few element the primary couple of times you exercise this meditation. Your thoughts becomes knowledgeable to pick out out up on these sensations over the years.

- When you're prepared, go with the flow right down to the complete brow region from the the front to the again of your head. Focus on this place—once more, noticing any sensations there.

- When you're equipped, skip all the way down to the eyes, then the nostril, the place above the mouth then the mouth itself. Spend a few minutes on every place and have a look at the sensations.

• Continue the body take a look at with the useful resource of transferring downwards and exploring every a part of your frame; chin, neck, shoulders, hands, torso, pinnacle of the stomach, lower belly, pinnacle thighs, legs, and in the long run stop with the ft.

• Do no longer react to or choose out any terrible sensations that you can revel in. Simply renowned them and flow into on.

• If you need, you can repeat the body test starting over again from the top of your head.

The meditation heightens the instinct with the aid of manner of manner of creating you extra privy to the subtle sensations in your body. You can also get maintain of high quality insights or "aha!" moments as you are meditating—or maybe days after the meditation.

Meditation 3: Golden Ball of Light

• Sit inside the lotus function or a cushty chair collectively together with your returned proper away.

• Breathe deeply and sense the anxiety leave your muscle mass with every breath.

• Visualize a heat go along with the float of electricity flowing through your frame from the top of your head down to your feet. Continue to visualise and enjoy this energy slowly circulating round your frame.

• Next, direct your attention to the 0.33 eye chakra and the warm electricity filling the space between your brows.

• Visualize the energy coming together to form a rotating ball of golden slight inside the middle of your 1/three eye chakra.

• Focus on the rotating ball and the lovely golden mild that emanates from it.

• When you feel prepared, permit the slight to extend until it fills all your 1/3 eye chakra. Visualize it growing slowly until it in the long run emerges out of your forehead in a outstanding ray of incandescent golden moderate.

- Gaze on the adorable ray of mild collectively together along with your inner eye and be conscious any colours or pictures that seem inside it.

- Simply renowned what you notice without judgment.

- Now, despite the fact that looking at into the light collectively at the side of your 0.33 eye, ask your 1/3 eye if it has a message for you. Take as an awful lot time as you want.

- When you're prepared, deliver yourself decrease lower back to fact with deep respiratory and slowly open your eyes.

Again, don't worry if you do now not see irrespective of the number one few instances you exercising this meditation. The extra you enhance, the stronger the ray of slight becomes similarly to the photos and messages from your 0.33 eye.

Meditation 4: Third Eye Awakening and Decalcifying the Pineal Gland

• Sit in a snug function and permit your body some moments to settle and loosen up.

• Close your eyes, take a deep breath, and preserve it for so long as you could, feeling the fullness on your lungs. Exhale slowly via your mouth.

• Bring your full attention to the 0.33 eye chakra. If it helps, you may visualize it as a small ball of light.

• Allow your senses to turn out to be vividly and simply aware of the entirety spherical you; any sounds inside the records like voices or the hum of electrical home equipment, the seat below you, the texture of your garments in competition in your skin, and any smells that would come to you.

• Allow your senses to simply revel in all of those items at the identical time as dismissing any thoughts about them.

- Visualize your 1/3 eye absorbing and processing all of these sounds, smells, and sensations.

- When you are organized, prevent the meditation through taking a few deep breaths.

This meditation can be practiced every day. It energizes every the 1/three eye chakra and the pineal gland and heightens popularity and the senses.

Meditation five: Mindfulness Breathing Cues

This is splendid meditation to keep you grounded throughout your day and regularly aware of your zero.33 eye.

- Choose a positive cue out of your each day existence, which include on every occasion you appearance inside the replicate or brush your tooth; even as your cell phone jewelry or you have ended the decision. It is probably on every occasion you look out of the window or concentrate a canine bark or a automobile horn. Just select out a cue that takes vicinity regularly for your each day existence—preferably, more than one.

• Each time they arrive up, breathe mindfully for a few minutes at the equal time as focusing in your zero.33 eye chakra.

• Repeat the workout whenever the cue takes place.

• This exercise lets in you to lighten up and ground your overactive thoughts at the same time as moreover checking in along side your 1/three eye.

Tips to Get the Most out of Meditation

Here are some suggestions that will help you meditate better. These aren't obligatory hints but truly beneficial pointers to recall.

Place. The high-quality region to meditate need to be fun and alluring, with as little noise or disturbance as viable. It does now not usually have to be indoors. Meditating in nature to the sounds of birds developing a song or waves sweeping onto the shore is a first-rate enjoy. The desire is up to you: surely a relaxing surroundings that resonates with you.

Time. It is awesome if you are capable of meditate at the same time each day; having a consistent meditation time desk certainly enables to ground your mind and creates a everyday pattern of time-out for the body and mind. Many people discover that having a ordinary meditation time desk offers them some element to sit up straight for throughout a hectic day. Their meditation time is a quiet, energizing haven from the havoc of each day lifestyles.

Position. Whether you pick out to sit down on the floor or in a chair, the important detail is which you are truly snug. The exceptional characteristic is one in which you could nod off in case you want you. Always supply your body time to relax and loosen up in advance than you start, as fidgeting for the duration of the meditation will spoil your interest.

- Try to smooth your thoughts. Connecting with the 1/3 eye chakra and receiving records from the higher plane requires immoderate clarity and quietness of the mind. This is much less difficult stated than performed, particularly in case you are new to meditation. The high-quality manner to hold readability is to live focused on the 1/3 eye for so long as possible for the period of each meditation.

- Coming out of a meditative us of a is just as vital as moving into it. Never just open your eyes and leap up. Always carry your recognition returned to the bodily worldwide slowly and ground your self with a few deep breaths till you are really aware of your surroundings.

- Take it sluggish. Each meditation ought to final for at the least 1/2-hour.

- Wear free, cushty apparel, and no shoes.

- Don't be alarmed at the same time as you acquire a poignant message or notion, out of your 1/3 eye. This may disrupt your recognition.

- Learn a manner to sit within the proper lotus function because it lets in the tremendous alignment of the frame.

- Turn off mobile phones, TVs, and other sources of distraction.

- Feel unfastened to discover extraordinary styles of meditation collectively with guided meditation and meditating to nature sounds or track, or meditation that consists of bodily movement.

- Enjoy the enjoy.

A calm mind really vibrates at a frequency that resonates with the frequency of intuition. The more you meditate, the more your thoughts will discover ways to turn out to be tranquil and quiet, permitting intuition to be heard extra honestly. As your zero.33 eye starts offevolved to open and accumulate strength, so will your senses. You will begin to amplify crystal clean notion, in addition to increasingly moments of effective intuition.

You will find out yourself residing greater within the present second, as those meditations are also super for enhancing mindfulness. These sluggish changes may be all of the motivation you want to make meditation a part of your daily routine.

Chapter 5: The Pineal Gland

What Is the Pineal Gland and What Are Its Functions?

It is called pineal because it has the form of a pineapple and is liable for the producing of serotonin, a substance that regulates our circadian rhythm and controls the existence cycles of the human body.

The pineal gland controls the motion of light in our frame and is placed below the cerebral cortex, in which hemispheres of the mind meet. Knowing the way to prompt the pineal gland, humans are extra open to feelings of ecstasy and concord. They may additionally have a experience of statistics the whole thing or a surprising information. In addition, whilst activated, human beings greater without difficulty amplify the functionality to adventure to awesome dimensions, called astral projection or issue declaration.

According to Theosophy, the pineal gland is a deliver of clairvoyance and instinct, in addition to a form of portal for higher dimensions, because the "1/3 eye" gives us perception past the limits of favored vision.

How to Activate the Pineal Gland

Activation may be executed via yoga, meditation, and different more esoteric techniques. Here is an workout that you could perform with out leaving your property.

- Sit with no trouble and place the index finger of your proper hand between the eyebrows, marking the thing.

- Concentrate on feeling a finger touch your brow. Try to sense the heat and throb at this thing for your brow.

- When you genuinely enjoy the pulsation at this issue to your brow, dispose of your finger and begin to deepen this sense on your head.

- Then begin to visualize the exceptional moderate coming from the top of the pinnacle immediately to the pulsating aspect in the center of the eyebrows and within the head.

- Concentrate on the sensation of stress at the point at the brow wherein slight accumulates and enters. You may also additionally moreover sense tinnitus and mild pain in the brow, which encompass stress.

With this exercising, you activate the zero.33 eye and start to decalcify the pineal gland. This workout need to be repeated every day or severa times an afternoon, as you choice. Little via using little, you could expand your clarity in dreams, intuition, and clairvoyance.

Why Is the Pineal Gland Blocked?

Researchers declare that the number one element that is chargeable for calcification of the pineal gland is fluoride in water. Also, chlorine, a low-nutrient diet, processed elements, electromagnetic fields (inclusive of mobile phones), and environmental pollutants are risky to the pineal gland, this is ultimately calcined with materials together with calcium phosphate, calcium carbonate, phosphate magnesium, and ammonium phosphate.

Activities and sports activities activities to decalcify the pineal gland

First of all, for this to art work, it is vital to avoid calcium dietary dietary supplements. Artificial calcium nutritional supplements are the precept motive of calcification. Now, commercial food usually consists of calcium in a unmarried shape or any other: calcium phosphate, calcium carbonate, or dicalcium phosphate. So do not eat "all finished" anymore, and make smoothies! You will see why.

Raw cacao: Raw cacao consists of many antioxidants, which makes it an high-quality purifier. It is likewise right for stimulating the pineal gland, the "zero.33 eye" and instinct.

Citric Acid: Squeezed lemon juice is fantastic for detoxifying your pineal gland.

You can combination this lemon juice with spring water; it is sparkling, and it's far much less horrible for the tooth due to an entire lot much less acidity.

Garlic: A garlic treatment is great for decalcification because garlic lets in dissolve calcium and acts as an antibiotic. Garlic is also top for the immune device. During your remedy, growth your dose steadily to a head of garlic an afternoon! To avoid terrible breath, squeeze the garlic and blend it with apple cider vinegar or clean lemon juice.

Boron: Boron is exceptional for detoxifying and cleaning of the pineal gland. It is also effective in putting off fluoride. You can try which incorporates 1/4 teaspoon of sodium borate (borax) on your green tea. A cheap source of boron is traditional borax, which can be sold in most supermarkets. Borax have to be taken in very small portions, in herbal water, and not using a greater than 1/32 to as a minimum one/four teaspoon of borax in line with liter of water. The safe and effective manner is to consume this combination in small portions at some point of the day.

Chlorella: Did you apprehend that chlorella has a phytochemical detail that can correctly rebuild nerve damage in the thoughts and fearful tool; in this manner, chlorella is used to get better patients with Alzheimer's illness and Parkinson's ailment. You can live actually definitely with the useful resource of way of consuming micro-algae like Chlorella and Spirulina; they're superfoods from 2 to 8 microns, so the scale of the blood cells.

The truth that chlorella is inexperienced comes from its chlorophyll content. It does not incorporate diffused carbohydrates, includes a excessive level of digestive protein, includes fatty acids, now not horrible fats, consists of chlorophyll. It is said that chlorella is a incredible entire. In addition to being a whole protein it includes all the vitamins; B, weight loss plan C, diet E, and the principle minerals (along with iron zinc in quantities huge enough to be considered complimentary), it has been decided, that it improves the immune tool, improves digestion and cleansing; accelerate recovery, protect in opposition to radiation, it allows within the prevention of degenerative ailments, enables within the treatment of sickness, and relieves arthritis pain, due to its dietary charge, and permits the fulfillment of many diets to shed kilos.

Zeolite: Zeolite is a mineral located inside the historical seabed and derived from volcanic rocks. Its honeycomb-fashioned molecules have the capacity to capture massive portions of pollutants of all sorts efficaciously and expel them through the urinary tract. It can be taken into consideration +++ clay. It is delivered in very amazing powder acquired with the resource of a unique micronization way.

For greater calcium, we're capable of moreover awareness on nutrients K2, which acts as a regulator of calcium within the tissues, promoting on one thing the fixation of calcium inside the matrix of the bones and cleansing at the alternative all the deposits useless.

Avoid all additives that include pesticides: To detoxify the pineal gland, the high-quality is to make a remedy composed largely of uncooked end end result and greens, but of direction, without insecticides. The meat additionally consists of pesticides, frequently at the identical time because the animals devour cereals or grass having had been treated. Some people recommend vegetarian diets to detoxify the body or to defend the pineal gland in the direction of probable risky substances. Yet some meats are nevertheless recommended, so a manner to control priorities?

If you can not pronounce the chemical call of a product, it is probably bad in your fitness. Among those chemical compounds we find out:

Artificial sweeteners together with aspartame (there are barely more natural sweeteners like xylitol).

Refined white sugar (to be replaced through brown sugar, honey, molasses, agave syrup or maple syrup, cooked wine).

Deodorants and merchandise in opposition to horrific odors, industrially produced

Dental mouthwashes (replace with saltwater, enough!)

Chemical cleansing products

Activate Melatonin Production

Melatonin: Although there may be no in reality conclusive proof, many human beings believe that melatonin allows cast off fluoride via the usage of growing the decalcification of the pineal gland, which facilitates to degrade present day calcification.

To produce melatonin, our body makes use of an important amino acid, tryptophan, that is extracted from the meals proteins we take in. Tryptophan is then converted to serotonin, as a way to itself be transformed via the pineal gland into melatonin, which the liver will then metabolize. Melatonin limits oxidation in all cellular cubicles, it will increase the hobby of various antioxidant enzymes, so it has an anti-growing vintage impact.

Tips to Naturally Maintain a Good Level of Melatonin

Melatonin is commonly synthesized at night time time, and its manufacturing is inspired thru the absence of light.

At night time, show your self as little as feasible to an additional of mild, that can lower or even suppress the attention of melatonin. Even try to avoid any mild supply (keep away from sleeping with a night time time time slight, as an example). The mild disrupts the production of melatonin. If you need to have a light within the hallway or the bathroom, use a mild that filters the blue spectrum. (Yellow mild bulbs).

The day, in case you display your self to the daytime, the production of melatonin at night time time time might be preferred.

Eat substances that promote the manufacturing of melatonin: melatonin is synthesized from serotonin, and this is derived from tryptophan, an essential amino acid. It is, therefore, essential to recognition on food containing tryptophan. What are they?

Parsley, pumpkin seeds, cheese, cod, parmesan, milk and soy, turkey, pineapple, eggs, dates, lettuce, bananas, plums, rice, corn, and oatmeal, walnuts and hazelnuts, tomatoes, potatoes, and purple wine are wealthy in tryptophans. It is, consequently, essential to consume those food regularly, as a way to achieve an top-rated serotonin stage. For instance, nut consumption will increase blood melatonin ranges in rats with the aid of a element of three.

The Miracles of the Nettle

In 100 grams of easy nettle leaves, has all of the endorsed every day contributions of calcium and iron, further to six times the RDA of seasoned-eating regimen A and four times that of food regimen C. Reason for which the nettle is to be fed on instead inside the morning or at midday than inside the middle of the night.

Some are unusual additives, along with choline acetyl transferase, an enzyme that synthesizes acetylcholine, and nettle is the most effective mentioned plant to very personal this enzyme. If one grow to be no longer but happy of it, it's miles evidence that the nettle isn't a plant just like the others.

Other Basic Methods With Which You Can Start Work at the Activation of the Pineal Gland

1. Take the most from night time time and day

For the improvement of the pineal gland, it's far very important that the time desk of sleep and wakefulness of someone does not pass off track. The most useful sleep ordinary for the pineal gland is early falling asleep (spherical 10 pm) and early upward push (preferably, at sunrise).

In addition to drowsing within the dark, it's also important to discover ways to maximize the benefits in the daylight hours - greater often to be inside the solar (or at least take a seat down through manner of the window).

2. Electromagnetic fields are your enemies

Electromagnetic fields hang-out us everywhere: we even carry them with us in our pockets (phones), spend amusement time and running hours with them (laptop structures). Of direction, such an impact negatively affects the development of the pineal gland, so it's so essential to apply every opportunity to live away no longer best from the bustle of the city however furthermore from worldly items.

three. Meditate whenever possible

Meditation is a effective workout which could change a person's lifestyles. It is scientifically confirmed that it has a useful effect at the kingdom of mind and the entire human frame, supporting to find out concord, to understand oneself, and to be distracted from the bustle. For the duration of meditation, hobby your hobby exactly at the pineal gland, at the Third Eye.

Meditate regularly and chant mantras. Singing motives resonance inside the nostril, and this resonance makes the pineal gland art work. The extra often it's far excited, the extra hormones of kids are secreted into your frame. The sound "OM" resonates with the fourth chakra, referred to as the middle of the coronary coronary heart, or the vicinity of Unconditional Love. The repetition of OM opens the path to standard and cosmic awareness. You can repeat it for five mins, 10 minutes, or some other amount of time.

4. Do yoga

Yoga will pay large interest to the improvement of the pineal gland because the pineal gland is considered to be the very antenna with which our mind is capable of understand the maximum crucial statistics from the outside. The maximum beneficial posture for the improvement of the pineal gland is Shashankasana, i.E., hare pose, because it stimulates the pineal gland and pinnacle chakra. Thanks to this asana, one also can decorate memory and consciousness.

5. Use such aids as crystals

Amethyst, laser quartz, moonstone, red sapphire, tourmaline, rhodonite, sodalite. In widespread, any herbal stone of blue, indigo or pink colors can be used to activate the pineal gland, further to art work on Ajna and Sahasrara.

Take the stone and area it the various eyebrows for 15 minutes. Try to take a look at it in conjunction with your eyes closed. Maintain a maximum attention of those 15 mins. It is superb if you may do this under direct get right of entry to to the solar - then its rays will skip via the stone into the pineal gland. Moreover, it's far going to be less complicated to pay interest on the mild.

6. Use aromatic oils to stimulate the pineal gland and alleviate the overall intellectual usa of the us

They moreover assist with meditations and various exceptional practices. It is generally encouraged to use lavender, sandalwood, frankincense, pine, lotus, wormwood. Oils may be inhaled, ignited in particular lamps, sprayed, or introduced to the bathwater.

7. Use magnets for cleansing

Just placed it among your eyebrows for numerous hours. They entice alkali and as a end result do away with calcium crystals from the pineal gland.

8. Forget approximately alcohol, nicotine, and caffeine

These stimulants interfere with the mounted melatonin production tool. The much less you devour them, the better for you and on your sleep.

Some drugs moreover have the potential to disrupt the manufacturing of melatonin - don't forget to seek advice from a physician.

nine. Clear your thoughts on the present day day moon.

The new moon is considered an super time not satisfactory for all types of undertakings however additionally for the development of the pineal gland. If you manipulate to clean your thoughts, you can feel how the pineal gland turns on and brings calm, stability for your frame and cleans it. That is why in yoga, the day of the state-of-the-art moon is of such notable significance: yogis are honestly committed to non secular practices, no longer being distracted even thru eating food and water.

10. Make it a habit to examine the sun for 15 mins proper away after it rises and at sunset each day.

Ways to Heal and Balance The Chakras

You have now understood the strategies to heal and stability your chakras. This financial disaster will cope with the restoration and balancing of individual chakras. If you apprehend that any precise chakra for your body is not functioning nicely, you can take the subsequent steps to smooth the blockage within the chakra and moreover balance the strength flow.

This chapter will not exceptional let you know approximately the unique equipment to heal the chakras but can even advocate some essential manner of lifestyles and behavioral modifications. By incorporating those changes, you can count on quicker restoration and a more stability in existence and your energies. You'll discover that controlling your mind and feelings ought to emerge as less complex and it'd be easy to remain pressure-loose and happy.

Root Chakra Healing

Lifestyle Changes

• Practice Earth Sitting and Hiking

To stability the foundation chakra, it is very important that you installation a close to reference to the earth because the physical element of this chakra is earth. You may additionally revel in ungrounded while this chakra gets blocked or out of stability. Try to be as close to the earth for some time every day. Earth Sitting is a tremendous manner to set up a reference to the earth. You also can skip for trekking journeys as that also connects you with the earth.

• Do Gardening

Gardening is a few other way to establish a deep connection with the earth. Every plant that you deal with on the equal time as gardening has its roots deep within the earth. You get to set up a direct connection with the roots. You additionally want to cope with numerous earth in the technique of gardening, and that also facilitates in restoring the balance.

• Increase Physical Activity

Imbalance on this chakra can make you inactive. Excessive and unexpected weight advantage is one of the thing-consequences of imbalance inside the root chakra. To repair the stability, it is essential which you encompass a number of physical hobby in your lifestyles. If your paintings consists of excessive physical artwork, then it is precise sufficient; in any other case, be part of a fitness center. Sweating each day is very critical to maintain a stability. If you are trying to restore the stability for your root chakra whilst predominant a sedentary way of lifestyles, you're up for a tremendous challenge.

•Try Walking Barefoot in Grass

Waling barefoot within the grass in gardens is every different way to set up a sensory reference to this earth. It is a very soothing and enjoyable exercise. There are numerous exceptional health benefits of this interest too. However, it's far extraordinary for recovery the idea chakra. After the walks, you'll sense greater grounded, rational, and robust.

•Eat Red Fruits

RED IS THE COLOR OF THIS CHAKRA. EATING RED FRUITS AND KEEPING RED THINGS AROUND YOU WILL HELP YOU IN HEALING THIS CHAKRA FASTER.

Yoga Asanas

There are numerous vital yoga asanas that might assist in faster recuperation and balancing of this chakra. Some of them are:

- Standing Forward Bend
- Head-to-Knee pose
- Supported Corpse Pose
- Warrior I
- Warrior II
- Tree pose
- Chair pose
- Supported Child's pose

Meditation

Meditation is an fantastic way to heal and stability the chakras. You need to awareness on the pelvic vicinity at the same time as you meditate and try and be a part of it collectively with your 0.33 eye chakra. Try to extend and settlement this area consciously, and that would additionally help in stimulating the energies on this chakra.

Crystals

Black tourmaline, blood-stone, hematite, obsidian, ruby, garnet, onyx, lodestone, hearth agate, pink jasper, and smoky quartz can be definitely helpful in restoring the stability on this chakra.

Essential Oils

Myrrh, patchouli, sandalwood, and spikenard are some of the important oils which are powerful in recovery the muse chakra.

Chapter 6: Sacral Chakra Healing

Lifestyle Changes

•Give Proper Vent to Your Sexual Energy

This chakra is pretty bent toward taking component inside the bounties of this global. The physical place of this chakra can be very close to your genitals, and because of this, the sexual strength in your body can emerge as unbalanced resultseasily. It is important which you provide proper vent on your sexual energy. If your sexual electricity is not getting the right expression, you can increase negativity. Your temperament can also moreover trade, and your social behavior can emerge as aggressive. It is crucial in case you want to have a balanced and active sexual life to maintain this chakra in sync.

•Explore New Things

This chakra loves to explore new topics. However, if the energies in this chakra are out of balance, you can display a loss of hobby in the complete aspect. The smooth way to restore the balance is to force yourself to do new topics. Try new meals, clothes, and locations. Change and variety will help in healing the chakras quicker.

•Try Creative Pursuits

This chakra has a excessive capacity to be innovative. This is the chakra of the explorers. It has excellent present day energy trapped internal. If you strive new and innovative matters, it can help in stimulating the strength centers of this chakra.

•Get Involved in Community Service

This chakra likes to live for itself, but this could furthermore make someone self-serving, overindulgent, and detached. All this stuff can cause imbalance. To maintain your sacral chakra in stability, you want to get involved with some sort of network service.

•Take Help of Reiki Healing

Reiki recovery is a superb manner to find out the blockages in this chakra and solve them. If you have got were given have been given superior distaste for the entirety all of a shocking, you have to are looking for advice from a reiki healer at once for help.

- Orange Color

THE COLOR OF THIS CHAKRA IS ORANGE. IT IS ONE OF THE MOST VIBRANT AND FLAMBOYANT COLORS. IT GIVES YOU A DISTINCT FLAVOR AND PERSONALITY. IF THIS CHAKRA IS OUT OF BALANCE, EATING ORANGE COLOR FRUITS AND KEEPING THE THINGS OF THIS COLOR NEAR YOU CAN HELP IN RESTORING THE ENERGY BALANCE.

Yoga Asanas

Some of the critical yoga asanas for healing chakra imbalance are:

- Happy little one pose
- Child's pose
- Downward going via dog
- Cow face pose

- Bound angle pose
- Open-mind-set pose
- Warrior poses
- Four limb body of workers pose

Meditation

You have to hobby at the vicinity truly underneath your navel whilst you meditate. Try to revel in the orange light there. Inculcate effective mind and permit cross of the repressed reminiscences and emotions.

Crystals

Orange tourmaline, sun-stone, carnelian, moonstone, and amber are a number of the crystals that can assist in recovery this chakra.

Essential Oils

Patchouli, rosewood, sandalwood, and ylang-ylang are a number of the crucial crucial oils that can be used to address the imbalance on this chakra.

Solar Plexus Chakra Healing

Lifestyle Changes

- Practice wholesome limitations

Imbalance on this chakra can also furthermore make you forget about approximately personal and expert barriers. The top notch way to balance this chakra is to begin education healthful barriers on your personal further to professional lives. Don't attempt to encroach the gap of others. The extra you comply with the bounds, the less difficult it would get to guide a wholesome life. Your sun plexus chakra may additionally even start settling down in case you convey down the competitive and encroaching inclinations.

- Sun looking

This chakra receives its strength from the sun and moreover illuminates internal you want a solar. If you feel low in electricity on this chakra in any other case you are not able to recognition on your responsibilities, strive sun gazing early within the morning on the time of dawn even as the sun is red red. It will deliver power to your chakra.

•Sunbathing

In the identical way as solar looking at, sunbathing is likewise in addition beneficial for treating the imbalance in the sun plexus chakra. It can even help you in removing numerous pores and pores and skin problems.

•Physically energetic normal

It can be very crucial that to hold this chakra energized, you maintain a bodily active ordinary. This chakra doesn't paintings properly in the parents which can be main a totally sedentary manner of existence. This is the chakra of the hardworking lot. Try to get concerned in a few way that calls for extreme bodily art work or dedicate a while inside the gym or play outdoor sports activities sports activities.

•Breaking the comfort region

This is a chakra that sets new norms. It makes you strive harder and excel inside the entirety you do. If you adopt a way of lifestyles in that you don't need to pop out of your consolation location and take new traumatic situations, this chakra receives out of stability. To maintain this chakra active, preserve taking new annoying conditions. Come from your comfort area and do subjects that you haven't tried in advance than.

- Yellow

YELLOW IS THE COLOR OF THIS CHAKRA, AND HENCE, YELLOW-COLORED FRUITS AND THINGS IN THIS COLOR WILL BE BENEFICIAL FOR RESTORING THE ENERGY BALANCE IN THIS CHAKRA.

Yoga Asanas

Some of the essential yoga asanas for healing chakra imbalance are:

- Pranayam or respiration techniques
- Bellows breath

- Boat pose
- Half-boat pose
- Sun salutation
- Cat pose
- Cow pose

Meditation

You can workout body test meditation and various respiratory meditations for recuperation this chakra. These meditation techniques assist in feeling the raw energy for your body, and you're able to get maintain of your physicality lots better.

Crystals

Yellow Citrine, yellow topaz, yellow tiger's eye, amber, rutilated quartz, and yellow agate can be very useful crystals for recuperation the electricity imbalance on this chakra.

Essential Oils

Rosewood, lemon, lavender, roman chamomile, and rosemary are a number of the vital critical oils for recuperation the imbalance in this chakra.

Heart Chakra Healing

Lifestyle Changes

•Learn new paintings paperwork

The coronary heart chakra is the center of introduction. If this chakra is out of stability, the wonderful way to restore electricity balance is to ignite the innovative spark in you. Try to analyze some new innovative paintings shape. Listen to tune, discover ways to play musical gadgets, drawing, painting, making a song, dancing, and all distinctive revolutionary processes to specific your energies permit you to in stimulating the power center on this chakra.

•Treat your self properly

This chakra may be out of balance if you are not getting due interest or care. Emotional balance may be very important for this chakra as it's far very sensitive in nature. To restore the stability, you must indulge your self in self-care. Treat yourself frequently. Give yourself sufficient of 'me time.' Don't forget approximately your needs for prolonged. Repressed emotions will have a completely negative impact in this chakra's electricity stability.

- Love a person

This chakra has a deep craving for love. Whenever there can be an imbalance in this chakra, humans begin feeling unloved, undesired, and unwanted. To keep this chakra in balance, love a person. It isn't essential to like a person specially. Invest your love into some thing. Love pets, artwork forms, passions, or humans round you.

- Remain brought approximately

You need to maintain yourself inspired to keep this chakra in stability. Negativity, melancholy, and remorse are some of the emotions that may ride the stableness of this chakra. Listen to motivational talks and indulge your self in sports activities that invoke optimism. Your quality mindset can help loads in preserving this chakra balanced.

• Do charity or social art work

Charity or social artwork also are first rate strategies to keep this chakra operating resultseasily. The more you work for others, the greater you turn out to be receptive of fantastic energies. You emerge as accepting in nature. This is a exceptional manner to keep the coronary heart chakra in balance.

• Go inside the wild

Spending time in the wild is a tremendous way to present your coronary heart chakra a boost. Nature has a outstanding healing effect on the coronary coronary coronary heart chakra. It restores the exquisite stability within the body. You have to take not unusual breaks from your regular lifestyles and move once more to the lap of nature.

- Accept new humans

This chakra works incredible while you're accepting in nature. Do not have inflexible thoughts on your thoughts about humans. Be extra accepting and embracing. Accept people for who they may be with out attaching qualifications. This assist you to in retaining the stability in the chakra intact.

- Green

THE COLOR OF THIS CHAKRA IS GREEN. EATING GREEN FRUITS AND VEGETABLES AND KEEPING GREEN COLOR AROUND YOU WILL HELP IN HEALING THIS CHAKRA FASTER.

Yoga Asanas

Some of the crucial yoga asanas for healing chakra imbalance are:

- Eagle pose
- Arm balances
- Camel pose
- Seated spinal twist

Meditation

A guided meditation that permits you in turning into embracing in nature is the tremendous for restoring the balance on this chakra. Loving and kindness meditation is one of the incredible approaches to heal this chakra. You must preserve your thoughts whole of sweet feelings while you paintings in this chakra. You shouldn't shape too many ideas to your mind as this chakra can make you imagine bizarre things.

Crystals

Rose quartz, jade, green calcite, emerald, inexperienced kyanite, and green tourmaline are a few crystals that would assist in healing and balancing this chakra.

Essential Oils

Ylang-ylang, rose, palmarosa, bergamot, geranium, neroli, lavender, and melissa are some vital vital oils that may be used to heal the imbalance in this chakra.

Throat Chakra Healing

Lifestyle Changes

- Don't lie

This is the number one chakra that takes you on the direction of intellectual and non secular awakening. It is likewise a chakra that has pretty some electricity vested within the throat. If you lie lots, the throat chakra gets affected. This chakra doesn't assist mendacity. You will not pleasant begin dropping the strength on your voice, but you can moreover start having intellectual clarity problems. The maximum critical manner to repair the electricity balance in this chakra is to save you mendacity on your day after day lifestyles.

- Develop the dependancy of discussion

The greater you may talk topics with others, the greater may be the effect of this chakra. Discussions with human beings help this chakra in becoming more expressive. Do not keep your mind to yourself. Indulge your self in healthy discussions with smart human beings. You will discover that your highbrow clarity have to increase and the impact of throat chakra need to furthermore end up visible.

• Work on the art of public talking

Public talking is the individuality of the throat chakra. A individual who has the energies focused inside the throat chakra may be a super orator. However, in case your throat chakra is not working well, going for walks on the artwork of public speaking will help you in balancing your throat chakra.

• Become greater expressive

Start expressing your emotions. The more you hold your feelings to your self, the more the load you'll positioned on your throat chakra. Don't keep suppressing your emotions. Speak your coronary heart out, and that could help in restoring the steadiness within the throat chakra.

• Sky searching

Gazing the blue sky also can be very useful in restoring the stableness inside the throat chakra. The light blue sky energizes your throat chakra and enables in faster restoration.

- Blue

BLUE THINGS ARE HELPFUL IN HEALING THIS CHAKRA, AND YOU CAN EAT BLUE FRUITS, AS WELL AS KEEP BLUE THINGS AROUND YOU FOR FASTER HEALING OF THE CHAKRA.

Yoga Asanas

Some of the essential yoga asanas for healing chakra imbalance are:

- Bridge pose
- Triangle pose
- Camel Pose
- Warrior pose
- Extended element perspective
- Plow pose

- Shoulder stand

Meditation

Meditation at the same time as chanting the seed mantra of this chakra 'Ham' can be very useful. Even guided meditations with visualizations are also very beneficial in recuperation the imbalance on this chakra.

The longer you meditate on this chakra, the better the outcomes may be. Your immoderate attention must be on bringing clarity on your speech.

Crystals

Lapislazuli, iolite, turquoise, blue kyanite, aquamarine, celestite, and sodalite are some of the vital crystals for treating imbalance in this chakra.

Essential Oils

Rosemary, frankincense, lavender, hyssop, and German chamomile are some of the vital vital oils that may be used for recovery this chakra.

Third Eye Chakra Healing

Lifestyle Changes

• Don't restriction your self

Third eye chakra brings to you massive opportunities. It opens tens of loads of lots of doorways in front of you to do the identical component. It allows you in looking at matters in a different way. If you start proscribing your self and questioning every motion, you would possibly located undue pressure on this chakra. Start questioning greater courageously. Don't anticipate with a constrained mind-set. Think in broader and wider terms. Don't think quite a first-rate deal your self, remember the greater correct too. Expanding your limits of thinking can assist in addressing the problems on this chakra.

• Work on balancing your thoughts

Third eye chakra is carefully associated with your mind and your mental faculties. However, while the zero.33 eye chakra is active, it'd need masses of hobby to channelize the energy. It is essential that you engage your self in thoughts balancing sports to sharpen your thoughts.

• Work on your root chakra

Keeping your root chakra sturdy can be very vital for bringing a stability in your 0.33 eye chakra. This chakra can thin the road among reality and creativeness. You can begin imagining now not viable subjects. You won't live grounded and might start making no longer possible plans. You may face troubles in managing energies spherical you if your root chakra isn't strong. If you need to keep your 1/three eye chakra balanced, you have to moreover paintings on keeping your root chakra strong and functioning.

• Don't rely on daydreaming

Third eye chakra may additionally want to make you delusional at times. People begin living in an imaginary global, and all that takes place at the same time as they'll be no longer prepared to deal with the energies of this magnitude. Your thoughts and body have to be organized to deal with the energies of this intensity. You have to prevent having a pipe dream and begin living inside the actual worldwide.

• Be cautious of terrible influences

Third eye chakra will boom your trouble of perception. This way which you begin feeling the presence of different varieties of energies spherical you. You begin interacting with them greater regularly. If your electricity area is not very sturdy or if your root chakra is vulnerable, you could get stimulated through those energies. It is important that after your 1/three eye chakra is out of stability, you still be careful of the form of humans and energies you have interaction with. You need to proper now start work on strengthening your energy subject.

• Indigo

INDIGO IS THE COLOR OF THIS CHAKRA, AND IT WOULD BE HELPFUL IF YOU COULD KEEP

THINGS OF THIS COLOR AROUND YOU. IT WILL HELP IN STRENGTHENING YOUR ENERGY FIELD.

Yoga Asanas

There is not any unique yoga this is more useful in improving this chakra. You ought to popularity on elevating your cognizance degree as masses as feasible. This chakra is greater associated with highbrow and non secular attention and plenty a whole lot less approximately bodily manifestations. Try to construct a more cognizance.

Meditation

You can do precise 0.33 eye chakra meditations for higher balancing of this chakra. You need to art work on lowering the have an effect on of horrific energies spherical you whilst you're taking a seat for meditation as your electricity difficulty can get prone at times. You need to now not fear whatever at the equal time as you mediate despite the fact that terrible thoughts are available in your mind.

Crystals

Lepidolite, sugilite, lapislazuli, amethyst, fluorite, tanzanite, easy quartz, celeb sapphire, and kyanite can be beneficial in balancing and recuperation this chakra.

Essential Oils

Frankincense, lavender, and sandalwood are powerful in balancing this chakra.

Crown Chakra Healing

Lifestyle Changes

•Give recognize to your elders

This is the topmost chakra that is associated with non secular reputation. If this chakra keeps functioning in a balanced manner, you'll be specifically expert, ought to have a recuperation contact, and own superb statistics. You must constantly live in a rustic of severe pleasantness. It is like being satisfied round the clock regardless of the state of affairs spherical you. However, if this chakra malfunctions, it can frustrate you. The first-rate manner to keep this chakra balanced is to recognize others, particularly your elders. When you display recognize for your elders, it fills you with humility. That negates the buildup of negative power.

•Be thankful

Remain thankful for the whole lot in life. Don't be grumpy or sad. The more pleasantness you hold, the extra balanced the energies in this chakra can be.

•Do more charity

The more you supply to others, the more you acquire in love and recognize. Whatever you deliver away is the real wealth you may earn in terms of spiritual interest. Therefore, it is critical to stay worried in charitable sports.

There are just a few physical methods and gear to stability or heal this chakra. This chakra is kind of outdoor your body and isn't controlled with the aid of the use of manner of bodily things. The superb way to hold this chakra balanced is to exercising yoga and meditation. Both those sports activities can help masses in retaining this chakra wholesome and balanced.

Guided Meditation Techniques to Open the Third Eye

As said out in the preceding segment, the 1/3 eye has its vicinity above the eyebrows. It is the only responsible for the visible talents which embody, seeing visions, flashes similarly to symbols. For you to boom the power of the clairvoyance competencies this is in you, you want to use meditation as one of the essential strategies. Besides meditation, you need to attention on your 1/3 eye so you can recollect the opinions that you could have. You want to make sure that the zero.33 eye is open if it closed.

In a few instances, it may not open right away, and also you want to invite it to open till it does. When it opens, you can experience calm, and warmth runs through your body. The feeling might be because of the opening of the body detail that become blocked. It ought to be unsleeping in order that subjects will run without problems.

For your closed to open, you want to be preoccupied with a super method to use to open the 1/3 eye. It is vital because it capabilities as an airy bridge to connect every the bodily and the non secular worlds. The soul is what makes you a completely specific and energetic individual, and you need to ensure there may be get right of entry to thru the hole of the 1/3 eye. It will release the higher information, and you may understand the studies you are having once in a while. The 1/three eye does now not function on its very personal but in connection with the hypothalamus gland. That technique that it will have an effect on some of your vital organic talents.

Opening your 0.33 eye is commencing the entrance to the statistics that is stored to your soul. When you meditate to open your 1/three eye, you will with absolute confidence have the fine non secular manual. Powerful awakening will appear, and you'll understand the prevailing in you that is approximately to take you to higher levels spiritually. You can select to transport the meditation way so you can open your 1/3 eye. It can be either in your very own or with an professional to guide you. When you're doing the guided meditation, the expert will manual you on a few steps to make sure that your eye will open. Some of the strategies encompass and no longer limited to;

Step 1: Choose a Location

For meditation to hit the number one target, you want to look for a place that there are minimum disturbances. A quiet area is all you need to begin with. When you're selecting the internet web web page, you need to ensure that you'll be normal. The individual to manual you on the meditation want to be like minded with you. Your body, similarly to the thoughts, wishes to get used to the area that you can select out. A role that you'll select out need to be in fee of activating your 1/three eye. That too you ought to do not forget while deciding on the vicinity.

Step 2: Choose the Time with an Intention

After you, through with the first step, artwork on the second step; that is, selecting the time that you will be going for the guided meditation intervals. You will need to head for the training each day so that they may be beneficial. The time that you'll decide to be having the classes ought to be cheap. You want to stay consistent on the time that you may pick out. Think of the time so that you can fit your needs fine, and your body, similarly to the mind, want to be unfastened and in a rest temper. You want to avoid scheduling the durations proper now in advance than or after the time that you take your food. When you choose a morning, it'll paintings first-rate for you. But that does not advocate that another time is not suitable. All this is wanted even as you pick out out any greater time except morning is you preserve consistency.

Step three: Make Some Stretches Before You Begin the Meditation Session

You need to make some stretches in advance than you visit the assembly because of the reality you may should take a seat longer in the room. You should have a more comfortable time as you meditate on a manner to open your 1/three eye so that you can apprehend the energy this is in you. When you do this any time earlier than stepping into the meditation periods, you can visit a deeper duration of your highbrow framework. You can strive bending over as you try and touch the feet for as a minimum a minute. You can stretch your arms above the pinnacle as a manner of exciting. Do no longer overlook to install your lower returned and make certain that your ft are within the air at 90 degrees with the body.

Step four: Position Yourself

Meditation can't take area at the same time as you're recognition. You want to undertake a sitting function in which you revel in cushty, and you want to transport your legs. If you find this posture worrying and now not cushty, decide to exchange and take one which isn't hard for you. A characteristic on the way to make you loosen up and recognition speedy to your respiration, similarly to meditation, is what you need to keep in mind. You need to sit down at the floor whilst you shut your legs so you will meditate higher on a way to open your zero.33 eye and get proper of access to to the hidden spiritual treasures. Your chest must be open and your decrease back immediately. Consider placing your fingers every on the knees or the lap counting on the placement that you may better. Your head desires to be upright and near the eyes lightly so that you can get into the region of meditation.

Step 5: Relax

After you undertake a posture that you are feeling snug in, the subsequent logical detail that you want to do is offer your frame the hazard to settle. Meditation can not take vicinity even as you are not cushty. Be aware of the way your body is feeling and if there are emotions which you need to art work on them earlier than the real meditation, try this. Make positive that your complete body is comfortable and equipped to begin the session. Pay interest to all elements of the frame every at a time as you sit down in addition to lighten up. Shift your mind from any fear that you may be having and be prepared to be aware of the prevailing 2nd. As you breathe internal and out, make sure you feel your frame expanding and contracting while you are taking each breath.

Step 6: Breath

Breathing is a essential technique in meditation. Be centered on the manner you breathe inside and outside and located your complete interest on how you are respiratory.

Take deep breaths every so often at the problem of 3 as you inhale and exhale.

Step 7: Empty the Mind

At this issue, you can begin focusing on the 1/3 eye, that's at the middle of the brow. With however, your eyes are closed, circulate your eyes on the path of the 1/3 eye. Throughout the complete meditation manner, you want to hold the focal point without transferring the eyes from that role. Remaining on the emphasis, matter number from one hundred transferring backwards however do not worry if you are not capable of experience the 1/three eye at that 2d. You can take quite some time to get used to the gadget of meditation. It also can even take longer to set off your 0.33 eye, however that must now not fear you. All you need to do is hold consistency, and with time all subjects shall workout session.

Step eight: Access the Third Eye

When you're via with counting from a hundred backward, it is time which you try and get right of entry to the sight. Make tremendous that you had maintained the focal point inside the previous steps in order that this component might be a success. When you have got the attention, you could phrase that all subjects are darkish other than your zero.33 eye. When the attention is energetic, your mind may be as nicely cushty and performing on a totally new stage. All the edges of the mind will work in unison, and you can feel the energy that surrounds you. You will enjoy a trendy strength diploma on foot thru your body as well as round you. That is the on the spot you may understand that to procure get entry to for your zero.33 eye. When you reputation on an object or image strongly, this is the time which you realise that you are getting access to the eye. Your thoughts desires to be fed on through the object or image genuinely for that to take vicinity.

Step 9: Work on Experiencing Your Third Eye

Everyone has a one among a type way of reacting to the activation in their zero.33 eye. You can also moreover experience your thoughts flashing visual effects and a few other memories and scenes that you may have come via. It may be a manner of seeing your mind much like the manner they appear inside the event that they may be laid out. As you hold focusing on experiencing your 1/3 eye, you'll paintings on starting the eye slowly through slowly.

Step 10: Maintain Your Focus at the Third Eye

You want to remain centered on the zero.33 eye for about ten to fifteen minutes. You might also moreover have a headache during the first actual periods however recognize that it is a normal issue with a purpose to seem to almost every newbie. There is not any want to get worried for the reason that headache may be no extra as you get used to the exercising. You should educate your self to in reality admire your 1/3 eye and try to maintain your popularity on one image.

Amongst the photographs on the manner to appear to your mind, be aware about one that making a decision to pick. Make certain you figure to preserve the mind focused on the brink of interest which you have made. When you preserve your recognition at the 1/three eye, you could find out it open slowly. That will endorse which you had accomplished what your purpose come to be at the identical time as you've got were given been identifying to transport meditation. Your 1/3 eye will open, and you could have a amazing revel in with the treasured gift this is in you.

Step 11: Get out Meditation Slowly

When you ultimately obtain what you supposed, the following factor to do is supply yourself out of the meditation. Remove your popularity out of your 1/3 eye slowly despite the fact that hold the relaxation temper that you have been in while within the whole manner. Your guide will will let you recognize which you want to be aware of your breath.

You can select to depend quantity as a manner to even though hobby on your respiratory whilst walking on bringing your thoughts from the meditation. Open your eyes slowly to cease the complete technique in the end.

In instances even as you need to open your 0.33 eye a few other time, exercise the above steps, and it is going to be simpler this time round. That is because it will now not be the number one time to try this. Work on making your frame experience higher as well as become in contact with the internal self. However, on the way to now not come right now, because you need to exercising the meditation approach, and it will make you visit extra heights. You may be greater in contact with yourself in addition to the energy in you and round you. That is the principle concept of meditating to open your zero.33 eye.

There are symptoms that you may revel in to expose that your eye is open. Once you control to open the 1/3 eye, you couldn't have self-doubt. You can also need to have a desire to analyze further to research more. You can be greater touchy to spirits, and you may see them on occasion. You might be wiser and will studies out of your beyond errors. The possibilities are that you'll be extra innovative, and you may feel divine inspirations more regularly. You will reap wonderful capacity, and you may have pleasure and enjoy a healthy existence once you could connect with the spirits. You will find out the sector a place of concord to stay in, and you'll admire your existence greater. When you finish the self-journey, do not be suggest but paintings to reveal specific friends with a similar gift with you the way of self-reputation.

Chapter 7: Meaning Of The Third Eye

The 0.33 eye is appeared as a supernatural and recondite idea of an invisible theoretical eye, that is generally delineated as located at the temple, giving discernment of beyond common sight.

You have a stoop. You stroll thru the wooded regions, and you could choose out among tactics. Your instinct asks you to take the right direction. You ring your telephone, and who's calling. You meet a person, and your guts show which you can not keep in thoughts this guy. You see a few thing visiting thru the room without any viable Intuition clarification. There are matters the 0.33-eye desires to do with. You can come into touch with this on the quantity in that you improvement inside the religious approach. The more the 0.33 eye opens; the higher can be the instincts. Sometimes you could anticipate what will seem in advance than it does appear. Let it take place! You may additionally furthermore bear in thoughts right now the manner it have to be, at the extent in which you need to mention. Let the zero.33 eye be so!

One manner is to open the zero.33 eye.

One gadget is to open the 0.33 eye. It can seem while you are prepared for it. At this spot, you sense a particular weight. It might vanish. Months later, it takes area yet again. This isn't always abruptly starting. It is an experimental method which could take a long term to finish. The 1/3 eye is for your forehead, above your eyebrows, but virtually marginally higher — the critical factor in your intelligence, your imaginative spirit, and your inner shrewdness. We can not physical seem like a watch constant at this spot. It's a keen eye. The pineal gland is associated with that spot. The 1/three eye opens at the thing wherein the pineal gland is activated.

If the 1/three eye grows in addition, you may see virtually with it later, and watch severa measurements — a exceptional and interesting piece of your non secular growth. You may moreover experience a tingle to your temple, or you can feel a purple, swollen spot in there. Some indicators open the 0.33 eye. You'll see specks, sparks, and so forth. Then you may be capable of see all of the heavenly attendants' strength as they glide about you.

Indications on beginning your 1/3 eye:

Your goals are slowly turning into precise, so you may first-rate keep in thoughts them. You experience snug. You recollect, like animals. You see animals. You regularly get the feeling this befell in advance than encounters. You concentrate stuff different human beings do not. You have visions, in any other case you believe subjects special human beings do not do. You need more of the ruminating. You have end up an increasing number of contemporary and full of modern mind. Anything you understand earlier than takes location. You apprehend on this life what your motive is. You have met your hold close, otherwise you experience driven. You pay interest the feelings of others. You dig on the atmospheres. Often, you've got a caution (instinct). You get a shivering feeling near your chakra within the zero.33 eye. You see the electricity flowing via the room (in some times)

WORKOUT TO OPEN YOUR THIRD EYE

Step 1: Sit without delay in a comfortable role

Stage 2: Take a few complete breaths thru the nose and ensure you inhale your stomach. What's more, breathe the air thru the mouth at that problem. During this manner, permit the strength go away the body slowly, to an ever-growing degree, until you're free.

Stage 3: Remember the spot among your eyebrows once you have got completed, and then a tad above them.

Step 4: Consider an indigo blue package of mild, experience it, don't forget it, right in advance than your 1/3 eye.

Phase 5: Take and keep a whole breath. At that thing, keep your the the the front enamel quiet, tenderly. Make a THOHH ...

(Thooowww) sound at some point of the whole breathes out. You'll experience your 1/3 eye shivering whilst you find the exceptional pitch. Rehash that during succession multiple times.

Spiritual Support

You need to take severa days to rehash this. It will cause you highbrow ache; it's going to die down, however. If you are not organized to open your 0.33 eye, you can rehearse for a long term besides. It is not going to take vicinity. So do no longer force it, yet without a doubt revel in what takes place. Take the time it takes. It might will be predisposed to be a prolonged technique. A few techniques take a few years in religious boom! What I am looking for to united states of america is if now not whatever happens, it's far similarly bravo. You simply are not organized for it, and this is high-quality!

WHAT DOES THE THIRD EYE LOOK LIKE?

Each has 3 college students.

We simply have a interesting and conceivably extremely good zero.33 eye, regardless of the sexual identification or strict (or non-religious) set of ideals. The trouble is a massive form of the 1/three eyes of gift-day are inactivated, "calcified," near, torpid, and unwakened.

The exciting records? Reflection is the commonly effective and persuasive approach for starting, arousing, and decalcification of the zero.33 eye within the international.

You do not need to debris with a sensitive ball of iron. Hurl the tarot playing cards out. Disregard based totally mostly on an elusive shaman providing you with the solutions you are looking for. What's greater, whilst you open up this new length, plan to unfurl a lifestyles this is an increasing number of conscious, vital, realistic, and considerate.

The 1/three eye is positioned in the pineal gland. While the pineal gland can be the focal point for the 6th feel, the 1/3 eye is appreciably more than genuinely getting ready to talk with the pineal gland.

The Third Eye is a feature piece of any person. One manner is to don't forget it's miles as a "meta" organ that consists of your mind and all your senses cooperating as a bigger, all of the more high-quality tactile organ that the pineal gland acts as a focus for growing a dream come actual. The Third Eye is a clever piece of natural evolution that helps you to see the examples of your existence. Your 1/three eye can locate the ones examples to you even more amazingly thru protecting the ones facts for your special senses.

Your zero.33 eye can be visible in severa techniques, as a reference. Soothsayers use their 0.33 eye to understand positive links and answer questions. Energy worker's 'experience' the energies spherical them, and then control that energy deliberately. What's more, each time you have got sympathy, you operate your third eye to touch and sense specific human beings's feelings. There are several excellent thoughts for the way human beings use the Third Eye.

WHO HAS THE THIRD EYE?

Every human has the 1/3 eye's information. It's for all and sundry in any situation.

A big range of human beings do now not benefit the Sixth Chakra due to the reality they slip via the snares in their personalities, transferring for economic rewards and dwelling at the physical component in their lives. Their spirits, anyways deep within, are edgy for religious pride. They just use their human imaginative and prescient, ignoring the metaphysical senses, and then turn out to be locked up in a hint region that obstructs the herbal global's intuitive belief.

The 1/3 eye chakra, but it is able to be, gives religious path in addition to allows for extended physical angles.

In reality, in numerous species, third-eyes were as fast as ordinary. One shape of reptile, the tuatara underneath chance, has a third eye that frequently captures. Other uncommon sorts of frogs additionally have 0.33 eyes that respond to slight adjustments.

It way that we're usually accepting lies for the facts, and now not locating the actual roots of our issues, getting wrapped up in our irrational feelings of trepidation that separate us from others and the universe. Looking terrible, proper? The problem is, we were given used to developing our identities near down.

The chakra inside the 1/3 eye conceals masses of capacities. It gives us a gateway to deeper facts about religious truths. It extends our popularity and the potential to upward thrust above human cognizance on the identical time as acted upon. It allows us to apprehend the fine degrees of our reality, and to put off the hallucination of social tips and restrained techniques of reasoning.

If our 1/3 eye isn't always completely open, we preserve to maintain in thoughts the divine realities and the arena's natural perception. Once it's far completely accessible and changed, we get the power to guide the soul to talk and triumph over the bounds of lifestyles.

The mind shrouds distinct powers that are not seen to the giant majority however may be applied with the aid of these determined to shore up their higher interest.

What Is The Third Eye Doing?

This vital, pineal gland positioned higher power trouble, stated frequently because the 1/three eye chakra, is wherein we will take gain of that which we can't see, flavor, bodily enjoy, pay attention, or scent.

This incredible capability for "sixth revel in" rises above our five maximum vital human senses, normally making itself recognized to us through hunches. It may be understood thoroughly that the 0.33 eye is aware about the mysterious and sees the unnoticeable.

With the developmental recognition of the single difficulty idea (that we are quantumly related with as an entire), more and more researchers encompass 1/3-eye belief as a real, legitimate wonder.

Is It The Same For All?

For positive guys, whilst the real eyes are locked, the zero.33 eye is attained. It should also be superb for others, too.

The 1/three eye can open, freely, haphazardly, or usually be open inside the path of contemplation or relaxation. The 1/3 eye is related to the 6th or brow chakra (energy focal element of perception, intellectual movement, middle, thoughts, beliefs, or mind-set or worldview). The 1/3-eye power is focused among the eyebrows at the temple focal component. It is most usually associated with mystic marvels in our manner of existence, despite the fact that right here and there, this diminishes the sacred gift it can be. It makes it excused excessively correctly via our left-brained clinical subculture.

Sight within the 1/3 eye actions all the time past each shape of vision you have got visible for your outer eyes or an internal inventive mind. The transparency and statistics that could very well be furnished alongside the tempo can be absolutely overpowering. I've visible such setting sun sunglasses, pictures which is probably vaguely outsiders, geometric systems which might be so hallucinogenic, and thoughts that language can not usually bypass on. They're just difficult to painting.

From an earlier time, you may see subjects into the destiny, internal our our our bodies, indoors spirits, and in reality indoors some thing. You can see differing measurements or universes. Now and then, snap shots are to be had in shading, quite contrasting sometimes.

What length of Time does the Third Eye take to open?

The zero.33 eye opens thru reflected photo. It does now not take lengthy for me to exercise. What you virtually want to do is consciousness your 1/3 eye on it. At that issue, photograph it being as excellent as a light. Do this each day for approximately 10 mins. Do this right now on for 4 days at that problem. Give it more energy as fast as in line with week from that factor on, however you need to apply your 1/3 eye, or you may lose the pressure and exceptional given to it.

One chakra is the "1/3 eye." The life-energy inside the frame (prana) or the recovery stress (kundalini) will feature on chakras. Know that if a chakra is enacted, any related screw ups may also be completed along any related "powers."

You can act in this chakra through the usage of setting your attention on it and retaining it there for some thing period of time you can supervise, with out interference. When you confirm that, you'll be displaying symptoms of improvement, and higher at it. In this situation, the location is prana, the essence of lifestyles — wherein the idea is going, it's far going.

When kundalini motives this chakra to turn out to be dynamic right away, you could have direct revel in of God (from an person mind-set in place of digesting Truth), the imaginative and prescient of the riddle moon, and the success of the terrific samadhi, and the regard of the adepts.

Why Do You Impact An Awakened Third Eye?

While the 1/three eye is most certainly linked to intellect and empathy, you do no longer realise of the element outcomes that might take a look at setting out the 1/three eye. It can reason awkward bodily sensations, for example. It also can make your behavior tough to manipulate, and at some stage in your rest, it could spark off mischievous stories. Things are what they are, does that propose that retaining the zero.33 eye close is smarter? On the opportunity problem, do the earnings outweigh the feasible prices?

Given effective premonitions, having an open zero.33 eye will purpose a extensive type of certainly one of a kind element outcomes.

Pay cautious interest to the subsequent aspect outcomes of establishing the 0.33 eye:

• A sensation of mild-weight amongst your eyebrows. This is probably like someone's vibe squeezing a finger delicately into the pores and skin spherical. This want now not take area while you revel in especially non secular. Yet, it is often a reminder that the non secular problem of existence is now applicable.

• Start picturing topics to your head (or perhaps begin taking into consideration actual sports) in advance than they arise.

• A feeling that the colours are greater beautiful and your condition is extra keen. An open 0.33 eye lets in you to take in the mild and the subtleties you'll otherwise pass over. From the outset, this will be excessive or overpowering.

• Feeling like you are essentially evolving, no matter the fact which you are not capable of articulate it. Because of profound events, it isn't unusual for the 1/3 eye to open or not appear lengthy earlier than the period of wonderful improvement.

• Migraines that experience like a weight for your sanctuaries or like a band round your head). Often this is defined, whilst the mind capabilities greater earnestly than anticipated after impact.

Upgrade social skills

Many people are prepared to brush aside intuition, in order that they allow squander their psychic capacity. None realizes that everybody has psychic powers, some more than a few, and but each person is unaffected. Such metaphysical skills can be developed and consummated; telepaths require constrained team spirit and meditation in location of internal to maintain their talents strong. Without following unique manner, even psychics might be residing in tension, as it can be. These ten levels that when helped them enhance their intellectual competencies and can now assist you:

1. Place your self in order

Negative thoughts block psychic talents. Simply be given as true with and stay peppy, too. You will achieve the dreams on time. Discover concept wherever and each time you can. Peruse recollections of these who've sharpened their psychic powers, and maintain to investigate approaches of emulating them. Remind yourself of any doubt you have. Just as the force of the supernatural, allow yourself to just accept as right with for your ordinary power. Anything that is less than a hundred consistent with cent of the initiative is unacceptable. During your spiritual endeavors, there is no location for questions.

2. Relax with a few try

To fall into an underground unwinding government, the big majority steadily ruminates or inhales on the identical time as focusing on naught. In addition to the truth that it clears your thoughts, however, contemplation adjustments cerebrum wave designs. This reduces the metabolic rate and soothes anxiety. It has eased high blood pressure and better coronary coronary heart health. Reflection regularly affects the prefrontal cortex slightly, taking superior intellectual overall performance under attention and elevating the pressure ranges – precisely what people want to speak with the non secular aspect of life. Unload the load. Only please loosen up.

3. Solve the variations with the ones round you

People can't agree to their spiritualistic items unless they discover a sense of satisfaction with themselves and others. Avoid warfare as all is meant to be completed, and rush to decide the warfare of your life. Find a way to compete, transferring within the course of the final desires helpfully. Only trying to damage every other out of anger really exacerbates one question. When you weight the person display in your shoulders, the reasoning is increasingly more tough; how on the planet do you easy your head?

four. Attempt no longer to take benefit of your highbrow capacity

Its undeniable abilties are satisfactory meant to beneficial aid guys. You need to decide the choice of creating suitable use of them. People who get narrow-minded with their uncommon competencies will usually lose them. For starters, if you guess cash through mentally imagining who will win bouts, put together to surrender your non secular affords. Nobody is granted control like this to win cash or a few element like that.

five. Embrace your troubles

Psychic contact can be alarming, similarly to big supernatural marvels. Yet despair is some distance greater disturbing than pessimism. When you still link to your divine side, you can not doubt the effects. You should are searching in advance to new stuff due to the fact you couldn't dare to dream. That's an enjoy detail, so appreciate the possibility you have been given. Consider all the subjects you can do for this sort of manage, and it does now not sound so stressful.

6. Consistently domesticate a Good Mindset

Do some element it takes you to be satisfied together with your lifestyles. This can recommend spending massive time now and then on yourself or having a leisure recreation which you experience. It all comes down to what is maintaining a smile at some point of. Stress and pessimism inhibit entire healing, that would help turn your popularity into the spiritual one. Until you could develop your intellectual capability, you can revel in morally free; you want to relinquish your doubts till stepping into a deeper nation of attention.

7. Find gadgets with a records you do no longer learn how to enhance your psychometric competencies

Touch the ones devices till the feelings are excessive. Attempt to connect with their records. Reflect for a few element amount of time you want to. Can you enjoy anything about the historic backdrop of things, or about their proprietors? Seek not to make your visions compelling. Just touch the stuff, and enjoy the way through the motion. Stop finding yourself squeezed. Avoid disappointment while feeling no longer whatever. This can take region at instances; first-rate one out of each bizarre entity has an interesting story behind it.

eight. Expand your creativity to boost your far flung viewing abilties

A an extended way off survey is a psychic capability to visit locations with out physical being there intellectually. Practice via visualizing which vicinity you anticipate to go to day after today. Something goes to exercise session of the store or the houses of buddies. Until resting, don't forget that you are in that vicinity. Notice the characters you find out for your creativeness, the artifacts, and shades. Observe which ones healthy whilst you are clearly going there and looking around. Record your fantasies to your mind to preserve them new.

9. Strengthen your telepathy via using attempting to pay interest the feelings of others

In whole tranquility, you can additionally impart your mind to others. Learn by manner of disturbing about how people say at some viable diploma. Have a person draw images or arbitrarily pick out out to play a card recreation. At that aspect, make experience of what is being drawn thru the usage of the person or which card end up drawn from the deck, but without quantities of records. Start doing those sorts of each day responsibilities. From the start, smooth-sightedness have to pay attention intensely, a good way to take a long time to growth. Over time and practice, however, it's far smoother and increasingly more reliable.

10. Praxis!

When you feel like you have got taken a stab at all, with almost no accomplishment, come back and ensure you have found each idea supplied proper right here. Everything well really worth prevailing is well worth having, so generally exercise any location you skip. Before you sharpen your capabilities to flawlessness, it could require quite tough paintings. Even inside the occasion that they do now not produce for a huge time body, they consider that they may in the long run floor. Put your inventory in! Ultimately, observe that the humans that deserve them are granted psychic powers, so they may without difficulty be eliminated. Do use your abilties for the excellent of someone more famous.

THIRD EYE CHAKRA

The zero.33 eye chakra is associated with the concept of 'seeing' in a psychic and non secular experience, mainly.

Having a powerful zero.33-eye chakra lets in you to apply your stepped forward inner steering from more effective, intuitive abilties.

The 1/3 eye chakra is correlated with advanced religious development, constructive feelings, and an mind-set in the direction of life this is more compassionate and charitable.

This chakra has a very strong relation to the pineal gland in the back of the zero.33 chakra. It come to be claimed that during historic times it turned into in which 'The View' is probably visible.

Ancient seers knew this, and they felt a 'tingling' feeling on this vicinity, too, as their abilties flowed.

Today's clairvoyants recognize this reality, and it is one of the many motives you may experience your psychic skills growing.

The 1/three eye chakra governs the present of psychic listening to or clairaudience, as this place resonates with the ears and listening to senses.

This chakra focuses on cultivating your notion, enhancing your intuitive talents, and boosting your smooth-sightedness and clairaudience.

The zero.33 chakra of the eye will art work to construct your inner information, concept, and actual reason.

Third Skin Color Chakra

Indigo, moreover referred to as Royal Blue, is the 0.33-eye chakra shade. This symbolizes a profound know-how and experience internal.

This color unlocks the Divine door, and it is the colour we relate to in the nighttime. It is at night time time that the senses grow to be smoother and extra subtle, and at night time time there may be awakening some other a part of ourselves.

Indigo coloration chakra gives your senses attention and includes thinking, listening, and seeing. Your 6th enjoy is what's called the zero.33 eye.

Indigo serves as a link among heaven and earth, many of the hemispheres of the left and the proper, and amongst existence and loss of lifestyles.

That shade permits you are making a transition to existence or dying.

The chakra of the Indigo dye is a beautiful exchange of shade. It lets you turn the decrease energies of chakras into higher spiritual vibrations

However, you want to be cautious, due to the reality you can become disconnected or unfunded with the life you've got and the human beings you care approximately.

Lessons on Crystals

You also can begin to see and recognize the styles as you open the petals of your 1/three-eye chakra.

You can see what locations you have got been, what locations you have got been stuck in, and in which you intend to go.

You begin having the moments of a mild bulb, in which the whole thing makes experience. You start to experience moments of clarity and discernment.

You begin seeing the developments, and you could be a part of it all to the bigger picture. You maintain to apprehend what all this includes, and the manner they will be played out for your life.

Illusions are shattered, and visions aggregate into your truth. You hold feeling the revel in of wholeness. You start playing a experience of quietness and inner statistics.

You additionally start to realize that with the affect of the indigo coloration chakra, you may consciously create your private lifestyles. All it takes is to employ a innovative act of will for your destiny imaginative and prescient to come lower back real.

The indigo coloration chakra is associated on a physical basis with the cortex, forehead, chin, jaw, nose, pineal gland, pituitary gland, and carotid nerve plexus.

People with immoderate energy from the indigo chakra get a colorful slight of their imaginative and prescient. Their eyes sparkle, and as you check out their eyes, you may experience deep perception.

It is calm but effective power that adjustments, transforms, and shifts. You love the top notch vision and immoderate metabolism at the same time as there may be a healthful deliver of indigo shade chakra through your body.

Your top body has strength, and there may be specific oral fitness, too. The spine is flexible, and so is also the thyroid gland.

The indigo colour chakra may additionally face demanding situations, which includes complications, vision issues, sinus infections, nasal congestion, allergic reactions, and night time time time blindness.

On a highbrow stage, the indigo colour consists of symbolic notion energy. Indigo 's 0.33-eye colour chakra binds the token to the substance further to the inner to the out of doors.

The indigo shade chakra symbolizes the direction of "handy movement." You don't impose your personal will or ego on the situation on every occasion you are in motion.

The movement clearly flows via you, and you get topics finished very with out trouble. You are innovative, and you may see what you need. You also can maintain in mind your dreams quite vividly.

You have an tremendous memory, and you may assume in symbolic phrases. You are innovative, and also you show staying energy and splendid electricity of mind.

But while someone obscures the coloration chakra, you be troubled by horrible take into account. You can also have problem speaking abstractly or the use of symbolic concept.

You experience caught in a single fact or truth, and also you lack imagination. You additionally can be insensitive and show off sociopathic conduct.

You additionally show horrible preference-making while something is disrupting the go along with the waft of indigo chakra coloration.

On an emotional foundation, the colour indigo chakra is responsible for the strength of the feelings. It lets you be at peace with your self, and it helps you very in fact see reality.

Indigo brings harmony and calm to the 0.33-eye chakra and the alternative frame chakras.

The indigo chakra coloration present is which you turn out to be at peace with yourself and the way your life unfolds.

You apprehend that not anything for your life need to be altered, that everything is proper, and that all is part of the Divine scheme.

The best hassle is that it gives as grief, isolation, excessive sorrow, or visions and illusions on the same time as the motivation is overwhelming or diverted.

But at the same time as the entirety is going properly with this coloration of the chakra, you grow to be extra intuitive, more perceptive, and in addition touchy.

You can join pics with emotions, and you are relaxed with one of a kind psychic evaluations.

The Indigo coloration chakra additionally makes you feel non violent and balanced emotionally.

On the downside, even though, even as it's far not in equilibrium, this coloration chakra will bring about visions, nightmares, and phantasm. You can also revel in anxiety flashes, which purpose imaginative and prescient.

You're going to be in a country of denial, and there will also be a few unhealthy obsessions.

You'll be distinctly aloof, boastful, or superior too.

The indigo coloration chakra non secular component urges you to upward thrust above polarity and beautify consciousness of witness.

You additionally begin to recognize the Divine workings at this spiritual degree and become one with them.

You collect deep notion and profound understanding. You moreover learn how to respect your mystical opinions and understand them.

You beautify your internal intuition and clear-sightedness and improve your divine remedy, too. You beautify your capability to go past polarity and unite your focus states.

But a few subjects can also have an effect at the herbal go with the flow of energy from indigo chakra to the zero.33 eye. You can not find out greater reality while this takes vicinity, so that you can not form a strong link.

You cannot get a witness point of view. You have dualistic and incapable of information the due to this of your instincts, divine belief, and psychic statistics.

You too are spaced out pretty frequently.

The hue of the 1/three eye chakra indigo binds you in your instincts and the non-public factors of you. It connects you to your instincts, on your intestines, or your 6th feel.

The photo with a Third Eye Chakra

The brand of the 0.33 eye chakra is lovely in its simplicity and is symbolic.

The brand of the zero.33 eye chakra is the Om, which is prepared above an inverted triangle.

The triangle is sat among lotus petals inside a circle. The sense of high-quality elements, at the same time as taken one at a time, displays statistics.

The 0.33-eye chakra is related to the Akasha element and ruled via manner of manner of the Om.

It's commonly blanketed in the exercise of prayer, meditation, or even yoga. It is a chant of Divine recognition, basis, and acknowledgment.

The photograph of the 0.33 eye chakra has elements normally related to statistics: the lotus flower, and the triangle the alternative manner up.

The upside-down triangle of the 1/three eye chakra symbolism represents the channeling of statistics into the seed from which intelligence rises.

When you look from the opposite course on the triangle, the widening sides represent your information growth, which results in information and enlightenment.

The lotus flower is a image of the universe, which means that that know-how. The lotus flower symbolizes eternity, fertility, splendor, and prosperity. They stand for loyalty, thriller, religion, and understanding.

Location of a Third Eye Chakra

The 1/3 eye chakra's function is right in among the brows, just a little above the nose bridge.

Contrary to common opinion, the 1/three pupil is not inside the middle of the nose, however in the various eyes in which the brows glide.

The 1/three eye chakra resonates with the pineal gland responsible for controlling biorhythms that includes wake-up and sleep-time.

It is a gland that is a attention of interest due to its relation with "mystical" reputation structures.

This is located close to the optic nerves, making this sensitive to adjustments in illumination and sensory stimulations.

Third Eye Chakra Traits and Characteristic

Vision and vision make a contribution to the 1/3 eye chakra. This is responsible for the information of power modifications and the implicit elements.

Besides, the 0.33 eye chakra is correlated with non secular powers, specifically clairaudience and clarion. It gives you get right of access to to magical geographical areas, in addition to enlightenment.

This chakra is strongly related to your belief and statistics. It gets your creativity and proposal prompted.

A 1/3 eye chakra is an device that helps you understand the subtler attributes of fact. It moves past the actual senses and into the diffused-power global.

Having the 1/three eye chakra wakened or induced enables you to speak in self belief to a extra receptive notion and internal vision.

Because it connects you to a one in all a kind manner of seeing and expertise, the 1/3-eye chakra's photos are typically tough to explain.

This chakra exposes you to the unknown and the not possible. Third-eye visions are more complicated than the not unusual visions, too.

We can look blurry, bubbling, ghost-like, or dream-like. But often they're smooth, like a film playing right inside the the the front of your eyes.

Maintaining your 0.33-eye chakra sensitivity includes awareness and the courage to simply accept as actual with in a taken into consideration certainly one of a kind way of questioning.

When you concentrate your thoughts and awareness, you could see through the delusions and obstacles that lie before you.

To create and stay a existence more deeply aligned together at the side of your most precise, you could have more notion.

The 1/3-eye chakra is aligned with the spirit international and the archetypal factors. It transcends time and lets in you to peer every the worlds inside and outside.

The 0.33-eye chakra power enables you to enjoy clean questioning, in addition to presents of self-reflected image and religious contemplation.

You can internalize the out of doors global thru the present of seeing. Using precis language, you could outsource the universe inner.

This chakra strength lets you attain your internal manual, from the depths of your being.

It helps you to lessen yourself via illusion. It permits you to benefit deeper truths that allow you to see beyond the phrases and the mind.

When you discern with the 1/3 eye chakra, it technique you have to see the whole lot from a witness or an observer's factor of view. It manner you want to preserve in thoughts of every 2nd.

Working with the 1/three-eye chakra encourages you to have a look at your self-restricting mind and to increase the facts that comes from the understanding that is going past duality.

It urges you to appearance and help others to find out the deeper meaning of lifestyles conditions.

In reality, the 0.33 chakra of the frame is holistic. Once this chakra is absolutely open, the thoughts hemispheres characteristic in synchronicity as well.

The gift of ingenious belief at the right hemisphere is blended with the rational and essential idea on the left hemisphere.

The chakra in the zero.33 eye is a seat of consciousness and a seat of moral feel. You will no longer best see what goes on to your international, but you can additionally understand what meaning.

This is in which your ethics and enjoy of justice spring from. When your 1/three eye chakra is open, you can no longer only see but additionally understand.

What motives an imbalance in the Third Eye Chakra?

Because of such a number of factors Chakras can grow to be blocked or unbalanced. They can be disrupted via experiencing an emotional disturbance or with the useful aid of turning into deeply disenchanted.

Fear, strain and tension also are common reasons for an imbalance inside the chakra.

When those blockages assemble-up, the strength glide thru the chakras will become disrupted.

Third-eye chakra stones are regularly sought by using people who try to avoid the ones imbalances. It is well nicely well worth noting, even though, that abuse of them also can worsen such imbalances.

For example, specializing in the ones crystals and developing your 1/three-eye to more can now and again make even the satisfactory intentions a bit unstable.

These same stones can, however, furthermore be used to heal, as an instance, from the shape of emotional damage that we're describing right here, which means they're able to deliver your chakras again into stability over the long term.

Third Eye Overactive Chakra

An overactive 1/3-eye chakra can purpose pretty a few mental and mental distress and be very disorientating.

You'll revel in like you are being trapped in an infinite sea of meaningless data and belief on the identical time as this chakra is in overdrive.

If you aren't well balanced enough, getting an overactive zero.33 eye will sweep you off your toes.

A not unusual signal of over-interest inside the 1/three-eye chakra is they indulge too much in the international of fantasy and lose touch with reality.

Another manifestation becomes overly preoccupied or terrified of visions of fable passing earlier than the eye of your thoughts.

When the 1/3 eye chakra is balanced, you can see all of this extra sincerely in your existence. You art work well, and you have were given a enjoy of neutrality in making picks.

You are concerned but no longer linked to a single very last consequences. You're truly targeted and you could parent between dreams and fact.

The everyday move of emotions may be emotionally exhausting while the 0.33 eye is in overdrive. You're going to enjoy beaten with the aid of the use of the need to take selections that would in maximum instances be rapid.

This lack of hobby, clouded judgment, and an lack of capability to determine what is right reasons this indecisiveness. These are all signs and symptoms and signs and symptoms and signs your chakra wants to regain its equilibrium.

Such clinical signs and symptoms and signs and symptoms and symptoms with an overactive 1/three eye include hallucinations, vomiting, troubles with paying attention to, despair, fatigue and hassle with the sinus.

There may be hallucinations, anxiety, paranoia, delusions and overwhelming emotions. Also, you may be judgmental and suffer from intellectual fog.

If you sense that once in a while the visions are too much to deal with you may constantly ask them to sluggish down and humbly say you want more time to accumulate and manner all of them.

When you worry similar to the energies you have emerge as exit of stability, lock yourself in your frame and push your self into the Earth.

SOME COMMON SYMPTOMS OF THIRD EYE CHAKRA

When the chakra of the 0.33 eye is blocked, it can occur as a feeling of being trapped in the every day grind with out being capable of see beyond the difficulty.

When you've got got an overactive zero.33-eye chakra and do not get assist from the other chakras, it is able to seem as hallucinations that sound manner extra intense than truth.

It also can occur as being no longer capable or not capable of realize this imaginative and prescient for yourself to create a vision.

It also can appear itself as a religious rejection of the entirety.

There's moreover a lack of readability and you can't see the larger image.

Third Eye Chakra Recovery in eight Stages

Overactive or underactive is greater than just the 1/3-eye chakra; problems might also additionally furthermore upward thrust up from a lack or loss of normal balance in your chakra electricity device.

1) The one-of-a-type chakras and their attributes can be used to deliver back the stability and heal the affected zero.33-eye chakra.

For instance, the sacral chakra can help clear out and ground your intuitive hits into your physical and emotional realm.

The chakra of the coronary coronary heart can also additionally even provide a more being involved and rational outlook to be able to cope with some factor that would damage us.

When you work to beautify the 1/3-eye chakra's capability, you need to live grounded so that you can permit the chakra's tendencies to mature extra genuinely.

You may be sweeping away your visions whilst you're now not nicely grounded!

You need to use diffused but positive improvements in thoughts-set to get again the zero.33-eye chakra equilibrium.

2) Continue your weight-reduction plan via adding nutritious components, and do each day exercising.

3) Energy healing, on the facet of sound treatment, herbs, aromatherapy, acupuncture, acupressure, and Reiki can all assist get the chakras decrease again to equilibrium.

These are sports activities sports with sturdy frequencies and first-class for calming the chakra inside the 0.33 leg. Just make sure which you interest on the purpose of balancing and soothing this chakra.

If the chakra imbalance has end up too large, it is actually some thing to do not forget visiting a superb, depended on strength healer.

4) Similar asanas will beneficial useful resource rest and recovery inside the 0.33 eye

chakra, whether or not or now not you are a yoga practitioner. That includes ahead bends, stands for the shoulder and pose for the child.

five) The 0.33-eye chakra additionally can be used with crucial oils. Take sandalwood, clary sage, rosemary, juniper, frankincense and marjoram.

6) Magic stones of the identical vibrational frequency or chakra shade as the 1/three eye chakra can also be used to remove the stress and positioned again the perfect go together with the float.

Stones and crystals which incorporates Quartz, Moonstone, Purple Fluorite, Amethyst, and Lapis Lazuli can play an essential characteristic in putting this chakra again into place.

7) Diet also performs an essential position within the fitness of your Chakra. If you need to have a healthy zero.33-eye chakra healed or maintained, count on indigo. Eat greater

indigo-coloured materials like kale, cabbage, crimson peppers, plums, and aubergines.

eight) Unleash the combat.

Your unconscious mind does no longer combat. In a completely aggressive environment, human beings with a effective, inherent person do now not thrive.

Taking a couple of minutes to examine your present scenario and take a look at if there are competitive vibes at artwork, to your relationship, to your administrative center, to your pals, or in your conduct that don't assist your inner properly-being.

Let move of the competing stress that consumes you and leaves you worn-out.

Allow yourself to live open to recuperation strength in vicinity of last yourself off because of the reality you do not even revel in the competitive energies.

Chakra Stones on the Third Eye

Wherever you gaze upon Earth, there are third-eye crystals found to assist therapy, maintain, and stabilize this all-important chakra.

Because the zero.33-eye chakra way lots to those folks who walk the religious course in lifestyles, it's miles constantly on our minds to preserve it turning nicely and in right alignment.

This chakra is constantly correlated with the color blue or red, however that doesn't robotically mean that the crystals which correspond with it need to in shape that.

Have an open mind as you undergo every of those pointers – in addition, we're going to discover how each of the suggested stones enables this chakra.

Indigo Kyanite radiates energies that stimulate the pineal gland and set off psychic abilities which can be dormant.

It is a excessive frequency crystal which has subtler energies that may balance now not most effective the 0.33 eye chakra but all the chakras.

It will assist the whole body in the energy flow. It may additionally even bridge any hollow in strength that could had been due to an twist of future or surgical procedure you could have had.

Blue Kyanite is the most common but Indigo Kyanite is the handiest to the 1/3 eye chakra.

Since the use of Kyanite you'll then use the 0.33 eye for one of a kind chakra stones.

The zero.33 eye chakra is the chakra wherein the non secular abilities can increase. If that is what you need to obtain, you ought to use greater effective and immoderate-energy, 1/three-eye chakra stones.

You can also moreover furthermore use diamonds made of Moldavite or Herkimer. Phenacite, Natrolite, Scolecite, Petalite, Satyaloka Quartz, Tanzanite, and Danburite are all incredible alternatives.

When you frequently use those stones, you'll locate new capabilities in case you want to start to appear, and you may understand a way to skip ahead.

Using medium-energy zero.33-eye chakra stones will help you flow to better-vibration stones until you are used to higher vibrations.

To this give up, you can use Shungite, Quartz, Lapis Lazuli, Fluorite, or Amethyst.

Fluorite will purify the air of mystery and upload greater useful charisma and Shungite will neutralize the energies emitted in the course of the restoration of the chakras. It will speak the suppressed mind, as nicely.

Lapis Lazuli might be part of you to a better fact and Amethyst will assist your intuition.

Quartz Crystals will make situations easy and pass your power upward.

Place the ones stones of the 1/3 eye chakra for your brow, and the space spherical your head.

If you are by myself and haven't any person to help make this formation, you could placed the stones next to you inside the form after which genuinely transfer and lay on them afterwards.

Close your eyes when you have completed with the grid breathe deeply and enter a meditative nation.

When you don't forget which you have won a better understanding of why the forces are trapped inside the 1/3 eye chakra, detach the stones of the zero.33 eye chakra and write down all of the topics you've got got learnt or encountered from meditation.

Repeat this workout each day, ideally at some level in the subsequent 21 days. Consistency and determination are critical.

HERBS TO ENHANCE PSYCHIC ABILITY

We have some of herbs to improve psychic abilties. Some are among us on the identical time as others are unusual. Forget the overall herbs that everyone maintains speaking about. To be a wonderful psychic you need to possess some form of empathy. So allow's first recognize how the psychics paintings.

What is Reading in Cold?

In short, psychic recuperation involves an electricity alternate. The depressed affected person sends their unfavorable energies to a medium, and the psychic passes the healing power to them in circulate back. That is why most human beings say they experience happier and more snug after a visit with a psychic.

Psychics hook up with your emotions through the strength that you are radiating. It's not continually about getting to be horrible electricity. Sometimes a psychic reads a glad going on to your life if that is what you bring to them.

Science furthermore confirms the complete psychic issue (for folks who do no longer take delivery of as right with). Energy can neither be produced nor lost consistent with nature. It just can alternate its form. Psychics are therefore parents which is probably remodeling and balancing those energies.

Psychological healers use three techniques:

• The spiritual treatment

• Curative pranics

• Curing the spirit

Some can check best one approach at the same time as others are professional in all three.

Whatever technique you use, the ones unique herbs can normally be used to improve your psychic competencies.

The Six Herbs to Boost Mental Health

To use those flowers, you do not ought to be a medium. Often we want only a hint little little little bit of steering to enhance our instincts. You want neurogenesis-inducing tablets and others that settle you down.

Wristband

This is taken into consideration to be a completely unique herb. During the times of St. John the Baptist, the plant end up carried with the resource of evil forces to electricity out spirits and guard them from abduction. In historic China, branches of

Mugwort had been hung up throughout the Dragon Festival to hold away evil spirits. Japanese used the ones to keep away disorder spirits.

A bed full of Mugwort in cutting-edge-day-day times triggers prophetic visions. During scrying ceremonies, we also burn this herb and drink a concoction of honey-mugwort earlier than the divination. Do I need to say extra?

This herb has all of the developments of herbs you need to enhance your spiritual capability. So the reality that it is frequently correlated with intense negative energy protection offers you the pinnacle hand even as interacting with robust powers.

Tummy

Turmeric consists of Curcumin, the detail it is answerable for yellow color. Significant neurogenic consequences are mentioned.

This herb is likewise effective antioxidant and anti inflammatory compound.

Research has validated that turmeric improves cognitive basic overall performance. Curcumin is used for antidepressants, too. And as an emotional, is not that actually what you need (greater recognition with 0 pressure)?

Ginseng-Ginseng

Both the American and conventional Chinese Gingsen versions beautify neurogenesis through activating stem cells to provide neurons. The herb additionally fosters cognitive characteristic and improves memory. Lastly, it moreover includes compounds that protect the brain, act as antidepressants, and feature anti-inflammatory residences.

Lavender

This one soothes wrathful spirits. See the way you fight traumatizing pasts with clients? Lavender must re-align your chakras and steer you in the proper direction.

Planner

Well, this isn't your each day herb. If you grew up inside the wooded area, this herb within the cities could likely never come upon. For centuries, plantain leaves had been used for restoration complications and shielding in competition to snakebites. This herb is also known as snakeweed, for this reason.

You must use such herbs as a medium to enhance psychic potential. First, plantain creates invisibility that lasts for brief. Without noticing it, you could sincerely skip its weedy timber. If you stroll the direction, you can take benefit of that power.

There also are regenerative houses in the herb. Healing wounds is believed to maintain flesh lower returned to existence. After a healing consultation with this herb, you can repair your cells and regain the energies out of place.

Frankincense

This herb allows healing by means of slowing down the respiration. You'll experience extended, regular breaths after inhaling that loosen up and relieve past traumas or issues. As a give up cease end result, the mind is open and free to leap.

Other than the aforementioned herbs, Blueberries, Omega-3s supplements, and Green Tea are also powerful in improving highbrow abilties.

How to Use The Herbs

Some herbs can be chewed in uncooked form, whilst others require particular techniques of software. Below are the ordinary methods in which we use the six herbs to boost psychological abilties.

Make use of diffusers.

These gadgets artwork nicely if there may be oil or a terrific powder for your herbs. Mix the herb with water, and flip the diffuser on. Close all the home home windows and doors, then breathe in for about half of-hour, relying on the temperature of the vapor.

The gain of diffusers is that you are feeling the impact nearly completely over exclusive techniques. Therefore, your airways are unblocked as you breathe wet air, and the sinuses related to the thoughts are eliminated. Clarity improves your mental skills.

Burning like an Incense

To dried herbs, this works splendid. However, you should mixture and burn coal or wood shavings with oils or paste from glowing herbs. Buy incense smoke ovens to make subjects a great deal less difficult.

Using Scented Spice Candles

You can purchase candles together together with your favored spices and flame them in a unmarried day. Some candles, but, have a low solid, at the same time as others have a much diluted frame. At domestic, you have to try to make candles, after which infuse them with herbs.

MEASURE

Most oils are infused with herbs for aromatherapy. Use the ones oils to massage strain points to enhance clarity, especially those positioned in the direction of your neck and head.

Food and Drink Use

Herbal teas are an regular use of herbs. We additionally use exceptional herbs in additives and condiments which include turmeric and desserts and pastries.

The handiest method is to release the aroma and oils in these herbs earlier than they are mixed with meals—roast dried seeds in a warm, warm pan earlier than they start splattering. For the leafy herbs, use a mortar and pestle to overwhelm them.

www.ingramcontent.com/pod-product-compliance
Lightning Source LLC
Chambersburg PA
CBHW071447080526
44587CB00014B/2027